Megan rings a fresh message for today's generation. She tackles the tough issues women wrestle with, including anxiety, depression, sexual abuse, eating disorders, broken relationships, and more. Whatever your story, you will find hope in these pages!

—Rebekah Lyons, author of *Freefall to Fly*

This is not a book for "nice Christian girls." It's radical. Prepare to be challenged . . . to examine your heart and break free from lies you've been believing. If there was ever a time to rebel and create a new culture that loves and follows Christ, it's now.

—Shannon Ethridge, MA, life/relationship coach,
speaker, and author of twenty-two books, including
the best-selling *Every Young Woman's Battle*

Be Rebellious is a raw, unapologetic glimpse into the minds of women everywhere. But it does much more than that. This book equips the reader with courage and inspiration to go against culture and do the hardest thing there is—totally and completely love oneself. When we can do that, what God can do with us is infinite . . . and that really wads the enemy's panties.

—Plumb, songwriter, recording artist, and author

This book is incredibly powerful and thought provoking. Megan covers all the hard issues women face today. I highly recommend *Be Rebellious* to anyone who needs to be inspired and realize their true worth is in Jesus.

—Nicole Weider, founder of ProjectInspired.com
and author of *Into the Light*

I'm *so* about this book. With an engaging style that feels like a conversation with a big sister, Megan confronts the lies the world throws at young women with solid biblical truth. She is starting the right kind of rebellion. Buy this book for your daughter and pay her to read it!

—Dannah Gresh, best-selling author of *And the Bride Wore White*
and *Get Lost: Your Guide to Finding True Love*

Be Rebellious is a truly incredible book. Megan pulls into the light every hot button of insecurity and fear. This book is a trumpet call for women to join together and claim the peace, security, and satisfaction that can be found in Christ even in the midst of terribly difficult challenges. What a beautiful rebellion against a dark culture that so deeply needs the light of His hope!

—Shaunti Feldhahn, social researcher and best-selling
author of *For Women Only* and *The Life Ready Woman*

Megan's words could not come at a better time to encourage girls living in today's culture. She speaks truth into dark lies and claims freedom for this generation!

—Kasey Van Norman, best-selling author and speaker

Megan invites young women to listen for a different kind of voice, one that acknowledges our innate value and refuses to compromise, that reminds us who we belong to. I appreciate her unfiltered anecdotes and unwavering honesty. This book will capture your attention and leave you hungry for more!

—Beth Guckenberger, coexecutive director
of Back2Back Ministries

Be Rebellious

be REBELLIOUS

MEGAN CLINTON

WORTHY
PUBLISHING

Library of Congress Control Number: 2014940722

Published in association with the Ted Squires Agency, tedsquires.com.

For foreign and subsidiary rights, contact rights@worthypublishing.com.

ISBN: 978-1-61795-108-4

Cover Design: Susan Browne Design

Interior Design and Typesetting: Christopher D. Hudson & Associates, Inc.

Printed in the United States of America

14 15 16 17 SBI 8 7 6 5 4 3 2 1

To my mom, dad, and my brother, Zach,
who have taught me to know and follow Jesus.
To my wonderful husband, Ben, who makes my life
beautiful and is rebellious to the core for God.
And to young women everywhere who dare to live
out loud for the One who loves us with an everlasting
love and goes before us as a rebel Himself.

Contents

Acknowledgments

I am very grateful for all the people God brought alongside me during the process of writing this book! *Be Rebellious* would not have been possible without the support, prayer, encouragement, and help from my family and friends. My deepest thanks to all of you!

I want to give special thanks to Laura Captari for her exceptional writing skills and remarkable ability to capture my heart in shaping the content of this book. An additional note of gratitude goes to Stephanie Livengood, who also helped me tremendously in the research and development process.

Thanks also to Ted Squires for encouraging me and believing in the message of *Be Rebellious*.

To the amazing publishing team at Worthy—especially Byron Williamson, Jeana Ledbetter, and Jennifer Stair—thank you for capturing the vision of this book and giving me the opportunity to share it with young women from all walks of life.

A special note of appreciation goes to my parents, Tim and Julie Clinton, for believing in me long before anyone else did.

Thank you for showing me how to be rebellious in living a radical, free, unhindered life for God.

I can't imagine what I would do without my wonderful fiancé—now husband!—Ben Allison, who supported me all throughout the writing of this book. I love my new life with you, and I'm excited for all that God has for us together.

As always, I offer my deepest thanks to my Lord and Savior, Jesus Christ. May You get all the glory for these words and use this book to encourage today's generation of young women to rebel against the lies of our culture and start a movement of hope, healing, and redemption through You!

Foreword

by Margaret Feinberg

No one challenges us like Jesus Christ. Through the immeasurable depths of His love, He constantly confronts the way we see ourselves, others, and God so that we become just a little bit more like Him.

When we are tempted to become preoccupied with appearance and possessions—Jesus grounds us in the truth that what really matters is our hearts, not the packages they come in.

When we are tempted to become judgmental and join the chorus of those who point fingers and marginalize others—Jesus shows us that our lives are better when we reflect Him to the lepers, prostitutes, tax collectors, and misfits.

When the temptation rises to make a name for ourselves, have the perfect body, or stockpile possessions—Jesus reminds us that none of these things will ever satisfy our true hearts' desires.

The taunts of worldliness always have a way of making us feel less than. Not pretty enough. Not smart enough. Not sexy enough. Not career driven enough. Not outgoing enough. Not thin enough.

We find ourselves snared in a tragic, never-ending quest for self-fulfillment. We end up settling—living anything but the abundant life God longs for us. Caught in the constant game of comparison, we lay aside our God-given identity as His precious children.

And we slowly wither inside.

As I travel and speak across the nation, I often meet beautiful, smart . . . and seeking women. Again and again, I see the hurt and the emptiness of not feeling good enough—not feeling wanted.

But what if we were created for more than fitting in to what the world says?

The night before He died, Jesus prayed for us—and His words are powerful:

> I do not ask that you take them out of the world,
> but that you keep them from the evil one. They
> are not of the world, just as I am not of the world.
> Sanctify them in the truth; your word is truth. As
> you sent me into the world, so I have sent them
> into the world (John 17:15–18 ESV).

In, but not of. Sanctified. Sent on a mission.

We were created for all that is good and holy. To become obsessed with making Jesus' name known. To love and serve in a way that leaves people awestruck. To inhale grace like oxygen and exhale hope to a world that is desperate for air. To live wonderstruck. Contagious. Radical. Free. Abundant.

Megan is a remarkable young woman I've gotten to know over the last few years. She's head over heels in love with Jesus. The love of God exudes out of her, and she makes people—including me—want to know Christ more. She's a delight to be around and is on the forefront of a new generation of women who are declaring, "We will serve the Lord."

As you read the following pages, my prayer is that you'll find yourself falling more in love with God.

Lord, I pray You would reach down into the heart of the woman reading these words right now. Awaken her to Your nearness and inexpressible love for her—more satisfying than anything this world can offer. Give her hope and courage to take a stand. To no longer live as a victim of her past, but to rebel . . . and follow You. To live a called-out life, sanctified by Your truth. Give her purpose. Hope. A fresh start. And a hunger for You. Give her eyes to see through the world's lies—and to embrace You—because in Your presence is fullness of joy.

No matter who you are or where you've been—if you've lived a life where you've seen it all, done it all, or feel like you're past it all—God still longs to take your breath away.

Will you join us on the journey . . . out of this world and back to His heart?

CHAPTER ONE

A Cruel Joke

I was lookin' for love in all the wrong places
Lookin' for love in too many faces . . .

—*Johnny Lee*

SUMMER NIGHTS AT MYRTLE BEACH . . . one of my favorite places. After a long day in the sun, I often grab dinner at Broadway at the Beach. Good food. Shopping. Lights. Energy. It's a fun place to let down your hair and relax.

That night, I couldn't help but notice her. Cute sundress. Way too short.

Add a little breeze and a Marilyn Monroe–style gentle fight to keep it down. Mix in a group of teenage boys trying to get a peep—and she gave it. Booty, thong, and all.

Careless with her skirt? I don't think so. It seemed pretty intentional.

I was stunned. Then she decided to lean up on a rail. I don't need to go any further here.

She wasn't sexy. She was a young woman quickly becoming a sex toy.

Desperate to be loved. To be noticed. She was buying into the lie that those boys really cared about her.

It's a cruel joke. In reality, those guys' interest has little if anything to do with her. It's just a booty thing. And she doesn't even know.

Or maybe she does.

The tragedy is, this tan beach beauty will likely end up in a series of empty relationships. From one guy to the next. Always searching, always hoping for something to fill the longing in her soul: *Tell me that I'm beautiful. That I matter. That you love me. I'll do anything—be anything you want me to be.*

When the guy moves on to another hot girl, she'll be left with a broken heart. Maybe a sexually transmitted disease. An unexpected pregnancy. An uncertain future. Confusion. Pain.

> We were made for relationships . . . God wired us that way.

Let's be honest—we all want to be beautiful. To catch a guy's eye and steal his heart. We were made for relationships . . . God wired us that way. We all want to be chased after, longed for, and cherished. I get that. I crave it, too.

But taken to an extreme, where can this lead us? Consider one middle-school girl's heartbreaking story.

Dying to Be Loved

Alluring. Modern. Goofy. And neglected. That's how Megan described herself.[1] A hometown Missouri girl, she was desperate to fit in. She longed to be noticed. Chosen. Loved.

But the kids were merciless. Bullying was Megan's daily reality. On the school bus. In the hallway. At the lunch table. After all, nobody likes the overweight, plain-looking girl. And braces sure didn't help.

Insecurity and self-doubt plagued her thoughts. She was trying . . . always trying. The latest haircut. Cute earrings. Edgy outfits. Another diet.

Then she met Josh. He was hot. He played guitar. And he really cared about her. Well, that's what he told her at least. They met online and soon began chatting during every free moment.

No guy had ever noticed Megan before, much less told her she was beautiful! She was smitten. Josh was the answer to her prayers! Maybe he was the "one."

She couldn't wait to meet Josh in person and was already dreaming about their wedding.

Life was finally coming together. Megan was getting her braces removed. She had lost twenty pounds. And she'd just bought a cute dress to wear at her upcoming birthday party. The dark cloud of insecurity was quickly disappearing.

October 16, 2006, was a rainy, bleak day. Megan stared at the school's clock, willing it to tick faster so she could get home and talk with Josh.

When she finally signed on to the computer, she was shocked to read these words: "Megan is a slut. Megan is fat." Josh had sent a public message to all her friends.[2]

How could he? Megan sobbed hysterically. *What happened? What's wrong with me?*

"Everybody in O'Fallon knows who you are," Josh wrote. "You are a bad person and everybody hates you. Have a &#%!* rest of your life. The world would be a better place without you."[3]

Maybe he's right. Maybe I am a horrible person. What's the point of trying anymore?

Angry and heartbroken, Megan responded, "You're the kind of boy a girl would kill herself over."[4]

Twenty minutes later, Megan's parents found her body hanging from a belt in her closet. At just thirteen years old, she became a casualty of our culture's destructive lies.

Megan's death was not a random act. It was the direct result of believing that life is all about getting (and keeping) guys' attention. When Josh betrayed her, Megan didn't know who she was anymore. She'd placed her entire identity and value in what Josh said.

And it destroyed her.

Turns out, "Josh" wasn't even real. He was a fabricated online identity set up by the mother of Megan's friend who wanted to get her back for being "mean." It was a cruel joke. Megan believed it, and she killed herself.

Many of us have bought the same lie that our worth is based on what we do and what others think of us. We've been tricked into believing that life is all about having a guy on our arm . . . and in our

> Many of us have bought the same lie that our worth is based on what we do and what others think of us.

pants. Sure, we all want to be loved, but culture tells us that the purpose of life is to find a boyfriend and have steamy sex.

And we're losing ourselves. We don't even know who we are anymore. This can lead us to some pretty dangerous places. We may not end our lives, but we are dying inside. We're casualties of a culture that doesn't care about us.

But we don't have to live this way. We have a choice.

Starving for Beauty

"There was a boy . . . and I liked this boy a lot. I wanted this boy to like me." As Melissa saw her crush walking toward her, she dreamed of all the things he might say.[5]

Do you remember those days? Maybe you're still living them in some way. Hey, I totally get butterflies when my fiancé flirts with me, and I look forward to a hug or a kiss. So I imagine Melissa expected something like, "You're really cool—let's hang out" or, "Hey, beautiful."

Instead she heard, "You know, you kind of have chubby ankles."[6]

Melissa felt her world crumble around her. She sometimes felt a little chubby and awkward, but to have her crush confirm her fears—ouch!

"That's the moment I knew I would do *anything* not to feel that way again . . . ," Melissa said. "I would do anything not to be that girl anymore. That's the moment I became anorexic."[7]

Melissa began poring over magazines like *Seventeen*, *Cosmopolitan*, and *Tiger Beat*. She was desperate for something—*anything*—to feel beautiful. If she had chubby ankles, no guy would ever want her.

So Melissa stopped eating, except for a few weight-loss shakes. She was determined to catch her crush's eye, only this time with a sexy dress and heels. When the pangs of hunger were overwhelming, she closed her eyes and imagined his reaction: *Wow, Melissa. You're looking hot! Want to go out this Friday?*

But no matter how much weight Melissa lost, she still felt ugly. And fat.

As Melissa's sad eyes stared back from her reflection in the mirror, she thought one thing: *You'll never be good enough.*

One boy's rejection sent her into a downward spiral.

Where do you see yourself in Melissa's situation? Maybe you don't have an eating disorder, but look closer. Maybe you can identify with her feelings of never being good enough, pretty enough, or lovable.

Can we escape these feelings of fear and doubt? Melissa's story didn't end in hopelessness—and ours doesn't have to either.

Maybe you can identify with her feelings of never being good enough, pretty enough, or lovable.

One day everything began to change for Melissa. Her best friend, who also struggled with an eating disorder, shared a glimmer of hope. *Why are we doing this to ourselves? I mean, if God created us, He doesn't make any mistakes, right? Who says we have to be a size 0?*

"God created you uniquely and specifically for a reason and a purpose, and He thinks you are a beautiful creation."[8] These words, spoken by a caring friend, served as a catalyst for change in Melissa's life. She didn't quite believe it—yet—but she ached to be more than ugly, worthless, and overweight.

Scrutinizing herself in the mirror, she sensed that God was saying, *You are My beautiful creation, Melissa.*

"I couldn't ignore it," she said. "So I clung to it like water and air. I made it my mantra every morning when I would wake up. I would look in the mirror and say, 'What am I gonna believe today? Lies or the truth? Am I going to be courageous? Am I going to choose real beauty or fake?'"[9]

Melissa is a rebel. She's rebelling against a culture that told her to starve herself to get a guy's attention. Instead, she's learning to accept and cultivate who God created her to be, and to take care of her body rather than destroy it.

A former vocalist and guitarist for the band Superchick, Melissa Brock is a voice of hope to other women, challenging us to open our eyes and see the lies that pop culture is telling us.

Three women. Three stories. All influenced by the lies of our culture. One emotionally desperate. One robbed of her life. And one, a rebel.

What about you?

CHAPTER TWO

Don't Drink the Kool-Aid

We all live our lives blindly believing in
the people who make the decisions.

—*Peter Høeg*

A S A LITTLE GIRL, I loved cherry-flavored Kool-Aid. It made my mouth all red, like the lipstick grown-ups wore.

One thing's for sure about Kool-Aid: if you're drinking it, you can't hide it.

As I talk to young women all over the country, I get the sinking feeling that we've all drunk the Kool-Aid, too. We've bought into culture's fickle lies about what it means to be a woman. And it's changing the way we live.

We've been duped. And it shows.

Our lips are cherry red, but our hearts are still thirsty.

Just think about some of the hottest TV shows out there: *The Bachelor*, *Saturday Night Seduction*, *Jersey Shore*, and *Mistresses*. Shows that are ridiculous and entertaining. You can't help but watch, half-stunned.

What we often don't realize is that behind these snippets of modern-day "girl life" is the encouragement to live at the whim of our emotions. It's about getting the rose at the end of the night and ending up in his bed. Like the women in these shows, sometimes we go to crazy lengths to be chosen and to feel loved.

What about music? Songs like Carly Rae Jepsen's "Call Me Maybe," Pitbull's "Give Me Everything," and Flo Rida's "Whistle." They are fun to sing along to—they've got that beat—but what's the underlying message? One-night stands. Sexual favors. Being a turn-on. Using our seductive powers. Is that what life's all about? Is that what being a woman is all about? Really?

And consider some recent chick flicks, like *The First Time*; *Crazy, Stupid, Love*; *Fifty Shades of Grey*, and *The To Do List*. These movies, and others like them, reinforce the lies our culture is telling us. The message is that relationships are based on sex. You have to look a certain way to be beautiful. Scandalous clothes gain attention. Sacrifice anything and everything to get *him*—the hot guy everyone dreams about.

Are these TV shows, songs, and movies entertaining? With their popularity soaring, they must be. But here's the tragedy: for many of us, the story line quickly becomes real life.

We identify with and feel a lot of what is happening in these shows, movies, and songs . . . and in some sense it makes us feel alive. Like we're finding our hearts—and more importantly, our independence and freedom.

Mistresses entices us with attraction, passion, and deception.[1] It's erotic. Sensual. Modern.

Without even realizing it, we begin to shape our personal values around these lies, unaware that we are on a pathway to brokenness and destruction. And the tragedy is we can lose ourselves in the process.

Without even realizing it, we begin to shape our personal values around these lies, unaware that we are on a pathway to brokenness and destruction.

We're letting other people define who we are. And Hollywood conveniently doesn't mention the painful consequences we must live with for the rest of our lives.

It's the girl who gives in to her boyfriend's pressure to have sex, only to find out the next day that he's cheating on her.

It's the college student who starves herself trying to get to size 0 because an ex told her she was fat.

It's the friend who turned into a party animal trying to fill her heart's deep aching to belong and be accepted. Only now she carries a sexually transmitted disease.

It's the woman who feels stuck in an abusive relationship. She would rather be mistreated and used than be alone. But she can't hide the bruises much longer.

It's the Barbie look-alike with breast implants and multiple face-lifts. Yet she still hates herself and feels like she's ugly.

It's the young woman, in a red-hot love affair with a married man, who stares in shock at a positive pregnancy test.

It's the girl you can't believe is dating *that* guy. She makes excuses and claims he's cleaning up his act, but nothing changes.

It's the thirty-something woman who is angry and bitter at God because He hasn't brought her Prince Charming.

And it's you and me. With cherry-red lips. Tainted by the lies.

Never Enough

We're always longing for something more. Always trying to silence the voices of insecurity and self-doubt. So we date a loser just so we don't have to be alone. We tolerate guys treating us like a sex object. We starve ourselves to try to be beautiful enough. We buy up all the latest fashions, showing a little bit more boobs and butt than last season. We might even turn to porn to numb our aching loneliness.

And why? Because we've drunk the Kool-Aid of our culture. We've bought into the lie that this is what it means to be a woman.

This is the cruel joke many of us are living in.

It may be entertaining on TV, but we're talking our lives here . . . our futures. It's no laughing matter. Behind the makeup and lipstick, we are dying inside.

> Behind the makeup and lipstick, we are dying inside.

The United States ranks among the highest in the world when it comes to unhappiness, with one in every four girls in America feeling unhappy.[2] And one in five girls admits to feeling lonely.[3]

Yet with 30 percent of young adults hooking up with someone they just met today and 64 percent hooking up with those they consider a friend,[4] we'd think our culture was somehow getting away from the loneliness. Isn't this how we're supposed to find happiness?

How far has it gone? Catch this. In a recent public opinion poll, 56 percent of girls ages twelve to fourteen said they think that one of the most important things they can do is attract boys and look sexy.[5]

With today's models weighing 23 percent less than the average woman,[6] it's no wonder 75 percent of girls wish they could surgically change something about their body.[7] And then there's

the mom whose birthday present to her seven-year-old daughter was a voucher for liposuction and a boob job.[8]

Suicide. Eating disorders. Depression. Cutting. Addiction.
Women tolerating abuse and being disrespected.

Really? What's happening to us?

Our generation is obsessed with "becoming our own person" . . . whether it's social media, fashion, tattoos, or drug use.
We tell ourselves that we're rebelling because we are breaking
the rules of our parents' generation—but in a strange way, we're
anything but rebellious. Instead, we're slaves, desperate to fit in,
living in bondage to the "norm."

Do you see it? More importantly, do you believe it? If you do,
there's hope. When we begin to see through the unrealistic claims
of advertisements, sitcoms, and
reality shows, we can make
choices toward becoming who
God—not our society—wants
us to be.

> When we begin to see through
> the unrealistic claims . . . we
> can make choices toward
> becoming who God—not our
> society—wants us to be.

I, for one, am sick and
tired of all the games.

I'm tired of the Barbie Girl
myth—the pressure to look like a model. To wear clothes that
are more like plastic wrap than true fashion. To worship physical beauty to the point that I'll do damaging things to my body
in the pursuit of perfection.

I'm tired of the Party Girl myth—the obsession with going out to bars and parties to pick up guys. To cheapen myself to being a sexual object for men's pleasure. To throw myself at any guy who comes along, for fear of being alone.

And I'm tired of the Good Girl myth too—that I have to be perfectly put together, never make a mistake or slip up, and hide my personality in order to be mature and be the woman that society expects me to be.

I say, enough is enough. I am sick of the pandering to innuendos and messages that put women in peril and bondage. If Kim Kardashian's seventy-two-day marriage and Katy Perry's fourteen-month marriage aren't what we're looking for, then we need to take a serious look at the lies we're buying into.

Living like the culture around us will only cause us to wake up one day in midlife, look in the mirror, and wonder why we're divorced or stuck in a bad marriage, why our kids are a mess, and just where we went wrong. Just look at Britney Spears. Madonna. Kate Hudson. Reese Witherspoon. And the list goes on.

Something is wrong here. C'mon, we need to all stop lying to ourselves and get honest. Sure, these women may have money, but it doesn't look like they've got a lot of happiness.

Let's stop drinking the Kool-Aid.

Let's take our hearts and lives back from a culture that really doesn't care about us.

It's time for a new generation of women who think, act, and feel differently about life and the future.

To be *in* the world, but not *of* the world.

We all desire to fit in—to be accepted and loved. But I say it's time to stop conforming! Time to stop building our lives on a bunch of lies. One of my favorite songs is "What Love Really Means" by J. J. Heller.[9] (Check it out on YouTube!)

She gets what true love looks like—not the cheap lie we've been sold. It's time to embrace our beauty and to run toward God, not away from Him. It's time to rebel against modern-day culture . . . and live free.

> It's time to rebel against modern-day culture . . . and live free.

Redefining Rebellion

To *rebel* means to "resist authority, control, or convention."[10] To defy established traditions and norms. In short, it's breaking the rules. Usually, we think of rebellion negatively . . . things like slipping out at night as a teenager. Underage drinking. Wild parties. Piercings. Pink hair.

Rebel and *Christ-follower* surely don't fit in the same sentence. Or do they?

But what if rebellion is actually the truest expression of fully committed Christ-followers?[11]

Could it be that Jesus was the greatest rebel in history? Think about it. If we lived in first-century Palestine, I don't think we'd see the "meek and mild" stained-glass images of Jesus that show up in many churches today.

Jesus' life and teachings were radical. Unsettling. Anger provoking.

> Jesus' life and teachings were radical. Unsettling. Anger provoking.

In essence, Jesus turned Jewish society upside down. "You have heard that it was said . . . ," He told the crowds, quoting their rabbinic laws and teachings. Then He went on to say, "But I tell you . . . " and offered a radical new way of looking at life (Matthew 5:21–48 NIV).

Jesus' teachings made no sense. Loving enemies. Praying for abusers. Turning the other cheek. Giving generously to the needy. Laying up treasures in heaven rather than trying to get rich. Trusting God with the future rather than worrying and planning. Spending time with tax collectors and prostitutes.

This was anything but conforming.

Scripture tells us "the crowds were amazed at his teaching" (Matthew 7:28 NIV). The religious leaders called Him a madman, a demon, and even the devil himself (Mark 3:21–22; Matthew 12:24). The Jews picked up stones to kill Him on more than one occasion (John 8:59; 10:31).

Why? Because Jesus was not afraid to challenge culture. He confronted the Pharisees' false religion and wrecked the materialism of the moneychangers' tables. He welcomed and valued women and children in a culture that viewed them like property.

He reached out to lepers, adulterers, and the rejects of society. He didn't hesitate to break the religious law by healing on the Sabbath.

And what was His motivation? Not fame. Not power. Not being the coolest Rabbi in Israel. Jesus Christ, our example, rebelled against the culture of His day to obey His Father. As He said, "By myself I can do nothing; I judge only as I hear, and my judgment is just, for I seek not to please myself but him who sent me" (John 5:30 NIV).

> If we want to rebel against the lies of our culture, then Jesus is our ultimate example.

If we want to rebel against the lies of our culture, then Jesus is our ultimate example. I encourage you to take time to read the Gospels, but not as a religious exercise. If we're really trying to follow Jesus—not culture—then we need to read the Gospels to see how He lived.

Jesus broke all the societal norms by teaching us to serve rather than trying to get ahead. To live fearless of others' opinions. To pursue truth, not popularity. To confront injustice wherever we see it.

Somehow we've been tricked into believing that Christianity means tolerating everything—being "nice" and looking past evil, corruption, and sin. Nothing could be further from the truth. This flies in the face of who Jesus is and what He calls us to.

Jesus wants us to obey Him. And people who obey Jesus are viewed as rebels, both by today's church and by popular culture.[12]

One Radical Woman

Not good enough. Ugly. Worthless. Dirty. Shameful. The words surged through her mind like a death sentence. Her friends and family didn't come to see her anymore. They didn't want to be "contaminated" by her disease. The religious leaders told her to get lost. Some even mocked her. That hurt even more than the constant pain coursing through her broken body.

The bleeding wouldn't stop. Hadn't stopped in twelve years. She'd tried everything. She wouldn't take no for an answer. So she spent her life savings searching for a cure.

But there was no cure.

"Watch out . . . here comes the bleeding woman!" I imagine them saying. Or maybe they turned the other way and pretended she didn't even exist.

Society named her an outcast. Yet she clung desperately to hope. This brave woman refused to be defined by her culture's expectations of women. Her culture expected her to bear children—she hadn't. She was supposed to care for a husband—no man wanted her.

In first-century Jewish culture, an unmarried, childless woman was worthless. And a woman with uncontrolled bleeding was considered "unclean." *Why not end it all?* The thought must have slipped into her mind often.

Yet she dared to believe that her life was destined for more. That her worth wasn't wrapped up in what she looked like or her ability to bear children. She didn't buy the lie.

Desperation gave her courage to rebel. To rebel against the labels, the comparisons, the jeers from the crowds.

How do I know? Because she stepped out in radical faith. To touch a man—a Rabbi, of all people. In that Jewish culture, her action could have resulted in death by stoning. But it was her only hope.

So she rebelled. *If I can put a finger on His robe, I can get well.*

They would mock her. Shoo her away. Maybe even throw stones. She winced in expectation.

Ugly. Worthless. Dirty.

She shook off those negative thoughts. *No, I am more than that!*

Crawling on her hands and knees between dirty feet. Choking on the dust. Pushing her way through the masses. Dragging her broken, bleeding body along.

She had one goal: to get to Jesus. He was her only hope.

Pulling together all the strength she could muster, she reached out and touched Jesus' cloak. *I don't care what anyone says. I am not worthless, dirty, and shameful. I am a daughter of God. He will help me.*

Immediately, a surge of warmth swept through her body . . . as if He had reached down and cradled her in His arms.

The bleeding stopped. It was a miracle.

Then she heard Him ask, "Who touched me?" The crowds would jeer. They would trample her. She should run. Get away now before anyone noticed.

But no—she rebelled again. Rebelled against the fear. The lies. The bondage.

"When the woman realized that she couldn't remain hidden, she knelt trembling before him. In front of all the people, she blurted out her story—why she touched him and how at that same moment she was healed."

No more hiding. No more running. I imagine the words came tumbling out, one on top of the other. Years of pent-up fear, anger, loneliness, desperation.

"Daughter, you took a risk trusting me, and now you're healed and whole." His words were like a healing balm to her soul. And in His eyes she saw pure love.

Cared for. Chosen. Beautiful. Whole. This is who she was created to be!

"Don't be upset. Just trust me." Jesus' words echoed back through the crowd. He was speaking to someone else, but the woman heard. And she smiled.[13]

Rebel. Trust.

Fears don't have to define us. Labels don't have to keep us in bondage. Life can be about more than running, hiding, pretending, always trying to be "good enough." We, like this woman, can step out in hope toward Jesus and dare to believe. He will meet us there.

Unlocking the Truth

Am I good enough ... sexy enough ... smart enough? Do I matter? Do I make the grade?

Who are you allowing to answer those questions for you? Where are you looking for your security and identity? Too often, we let boyfriends, movies, music, and models tell us who we are ... or who we aren't.

> Why are we trying so hard to fit in when God created us to stand out?

And sometimes I wonder, *Why are we trying so hard to fit in when God created us to stand out?*

God has a lot to say about our unique beauty as women.

Let's start with 1 Samuel 16:7: "Looks aren't everything. Don't be impressed with his looks and stature. . . . GOD judges persons differently than humans do. Men and women look at the face; GOD looks into the heart."

Ouch. How many times do you catch yourself defining your worth by what you see in the mirror—feeling down on yourself because of a zit or a bad hair day? Sometimes I catch myself wondering what my fiancé or best friend would think of how I look.

Does this blue shirt make my eyes pop? Would my friend say, "Megan, love the shirt! Where'd you get it?" Then I smile and shake my head at my internal war. I look in the mirror and decide to wear the blue shirt because I like it. It's comfortable and cute.

Don't get me wrong. I love my heels and pearls and MAC makeup. I'm not saying we should "let our-selves go" and not take care of our bodies. On the contrary, I think that's an import-ant part of being a woman. But I want to rebel against the idea that I am nothing more than my looks.

> I want to rebel against the idea that I am nothing more than my looks.

Here's what God wants for us: People "will be captivated by your life of holy beauty. What matters is not your outer appear-ance—the styling of your hair, the jewelry you wear, the cut of your clothes—but your inner disposition. Cultivate inner beauty, the gentle, gracious kind that God delights in" (1 Peter 3:2–4).

How easy it is to neglect inner beauty with all our focus on outer beauty! We make sure every hair is in place and our clothes, shoes, and purse match perfectly. It doesn't matter that we're falling apart inside if our mascara's not running and eye-liner's not smeared—right?

Nope. That's another lie. God looks at the heart. It's like He's saying, *I love you even when your hair's a wreck and you lost your makeup bag. I think you're beautiful. I created you. What matters most is your heart, not your heels. So dress up and get your nails*

done, but don't put your identity there. You are Mine, My precious
daughter. Don't buy the lies that culture tells you! You are worth
so much more . . .

We all struggle with insecurity—I think it's part of the curse!
And it starts so young. I remember in second grade coming
home from school heartbroken because I realized I was the tini-
est girl in the whole class. I think some of the other girls were
reminding me of that too! My dad wrapped his arms around me
and whispered in my ear, "But I love you."

As a seven-year-old, I giggled and ran off to play. But years
later, that same ache of insecurity still creeps in. I have to bring
my wayward heart back to the truth on a daily basis.

We have been knit together by God's hands (Psalm
139:13 NIV). He's known us since before we were born. He
custom-fashioned each of us to be uniquely beautiful. And He
longs for us to relax and enjoy being His daughters.

God's Word challenges us, "Don't become so well-adjusted
to your culture that you fit into it without even thinking. Instead,
fix your attention on God. You'll be changed from the inside
out. . . . Unlike the culture around you, always dragging you
down to its level of immaturity, God brings the best out of you,
develops well-formed maturity in you" (Romans 12:2).

If we try to fit in, we'll be dragged down into the muck and
mire of our culture's lies. And we've already seen the painful
places that choice can make us end up. So what's the alternative?

Fix your attention on God. Just like the desperate woman reached out to Jesus, we too must push through the crowd of our insecurities and fears to find the truth.

"Don't be upset. Just trust me," Jesus says. Can you hear Him? He knows your name. He knows your story. He is reaching toward you.

What will you do with the opportunity He is giving you?

Just like the desperate woman reached out to Jesus, we too must push through the crowd of our insecurities and fears to find the truth.

CHAPTER THREE

No Longer a Victim

Suffering, failure, loneliness, sorrow,
discouragement, and death will be
part of your journey, but the Kingdom
of God will conquer all these horrors.
No evil can resist grace forever.

—*Brennan Manning*

ALL-STAR SOCCER PLAYER. Homecoming queen. Straight-A student. Gorgeous. Smart. Athletic. Popular. She had it all. Or so it seemed.

Mo was living the dream. She broke every goalkeeping record at her university and was on her way to the top. "No one saw that inside I was broken," Mo shared. "Shattered. Desperately striving."[1]

There's no place like competitive athletics to feel the pressure of our culture's expectations. And Mo was quickly sucked in.

She was only as good as her last game. Her last grade. Her last rating.

Even in the midst of Mo's battle with bulimia, her parents stood by her through it all, loving and supporting her. She said, "My dad was my biggest fan. My hero. My confidant. My best friend."[2]

And then, one day, he was gone.

On January 3, 2009, Mo came home to find her family in chaos. Her father was missing. Confusion. Tears. Desperate phone calls. Unanswered questions.

Hours later, she woke up from a fitful sleep to her mom's screams.

Her mother had found a crumpled suicide note with his signature.

Policemen. Ringing phones. Her heart thumping loudly. So much noise. She saw the officers walking her way. Their news changed her life forever.

Mo's dad had put a gun to his heart and pulled the trigger. He was dead. Gone. Forever.

"My world froze. . . . I felt a numbness overwhelm my body and expand in the crevices of my being," Mo remembered.[3]

Her world was shattered. Her "perfect" life destroyed.

And Mo ran. Angry at God. Crippled by deep depression. Clinging to anything that would numb the pain and fill the void.

Alcohol. Partying. Boys. "I was confused. Torn. . . . So overwhelmed by pain, that I began seeking attention and love from all the wrong sources. I began clinging to anything that would offer me temporary pleasure and relief," Mo said, looking back.[4]

Driving home late one night a year later, Mo found herself talking to God. "I wanna trust You, but I don't. Reveal Yourself to me. If You love me like You say You do . . . why have You allowed me to hurt like this? I just don't trust You."[5]

Seconds later, Mo lost control. Her Jeep swerved into the center median, shot across the road, and hit an embankment. The car flipped three times. Wrapped itself around a tree.

It was 1:30 a.m. Mo woke up hanging upside down from her seat belt, coughing up blood. Completely and utterly alone and vulnerable.

Every rib on the left side of Mo's body was broken. She broke her neck and damaged her lungs and liver. Worst of all, she had suffered brain damage. In the midst of this complete physical brokenness, and still carrying the wounds of her father's death a year earlier, Mo found God. "I felt God, and I knew Him. He had interrupted my life."[6]

Providentially, there was a man on the road that night who witnessed the crash from a distance. When he found her amid the wreckage of the twisted Jeep, he heard her repeating one phrase: "God is beautiful. God is beautiful."

Mo was broken. Not just emotionally but physically. And after the crash, she rebelled. She rebelled against the lie that her identity was in how well she performed on the soccer field or how many eyes she could turn in the hallway. She rebelled against the hopelessness of her father's death and refused to let it destroy her future. She rebelled against the lie of control. And most importantly, she rebelled against the victim mentality that turns hurt into hatred and brokenness into bitterness.

"The majority of my life has been an absolute battle for control with God. . . . I wanted to call the shots. I wanted to map out my future. And I really lost myself in the process. I had to fail time and time again. But through all these failures and all this pain, God was there. Patiently waiting for me to see Him in the stands."[7]

Mo tried to ignore God. Run away. Escape. Define her own future. But she was stuck in pain, brokenness, and confusion. She bought into the world's promises of fame, fortune, and pleasure, hoping it would soothe her heartbreak and pain.

Yet there's no escaping our heavenly Father's love and pursuit.

> There's no escaping our heavenly Father's love and pursuit.

Stuck in the Past

Maybe you feel that way too. Broken. Weak. Unable to go on. Stuck in the past. Maybe depression has wrapped itself around your heart. Your boyfriend dumped you instead of slipping a ring on your finger.

Maybe your best friend committed suicide. Your parents' divorce left you spiraling and feeling alone. Sexual abuse shattered your identity, causing you to question everything. The abortion you had still haunts your dreams.

Or maybe it's an old wound. Your dad walked out. You didn't make the cheerleading squad. You tripped at the dance recital. A boy called you fat. The kids' heartless taunts still echo in your mind.

Stupid. Fat. Ugly. Not good enough. The thoughts play in your mind like a broken record.

Perhaps you, like Mo, feel broken. Inadequate. Ruined. Maybe the pain is so great that you'll do anything to numb it. Cut your arms. Starve yourself. Throw yourself at guys. Drink yourself into oblivion. Get high . . . just one more time.

No one escapes. We may try to hide it, but we're all wounded in one way or another. Maybe it's physically. Emotionally. Mentally. Spiritually.

> We may try to hide it, but we're all wounded in one way or another.

It's not a question of *if*. It's a question of *how*. And a question of what we'll do with it. Brokenness is all around us. At least seventy million Americans say their pasts hold them back from achieving their goals. And nearly one-third of us admit to dealing with unresolved emotional pain or conflict in our lives.[8] (The rest of those surveyed must have been in denial!)

We may try to hide our pain behind our makeup or our fashion, but here's the reality:

- *Sexual abuse:* One in every four women.[9]
- *Rape:* One in every five women.[10]
- *Abortion:* Nearly one in every three women.[11]
- *Domestic violence:* One in every four women.[12]
- *Clinical depression:* One in every eight women.[13]
- *Eating disorders:* One in every four college-aged women.[14]
- *Sexually transmitted diseases:* One in every two sexually active twenty-five-year-olds.[15]
- *Suicide:* The fifteenth leading cause of death among women.[16]

Pain is very real. And when we get hurt, we easily close our spirits. We wake up every day scowling at the alarm clock. We stop living and just exist. Just try to make it through another day . . . another week. It's a living nightmare.

"I'm stuck," we tell ourselves. "This is the way I am, and I can't get out." We buy the lie of hopelessness. We begin to let our past and our pain define us, driving us to dark places.

This is the life of a victim.

The world tells us to paste a smile on our face and just push through. But maybe you're tired of that show. Maybe you want to scream, "I'm dying inside and nobody knows it but me!"

The more you "stuff" your pain, the more poison seeps through your veins, your heart, and out in your life. Will you dare to believe that you were created for more?

More than a victim.

When I find myself irritated, angry, and hurt, I try to stop and ask myself: *Megan, are you going to let this get to you? Are you going to stay stuck in anger, defeat, and discouragement? Or are you going to choose to draw out the beauty? To look for the good? To rise above?*

I'm learning that we have a choice. A choice about how to respond to the pain and brokenness in our lives. We can't undo our past—and it does no good to "stuff" it and pretend it doesn't exist—but we don't have to live in bondage to guilt, regret, and self-hatred either.

We've all met women like that. Women who have let their pain beat them. They are victims of their past. Cynical. Angry. Cut off. Broken. Empty. Searching. Is that what you want . . . fifteen, twenty years from now?

Not me.

How much better it would be to take the risk to be honest—and then support each other on the journey of healing and growth!

There is freedom. There is hope. We are not victims; we are God's daughters. And He has not left us on our own. He is pursuing us. Calling us back to Him. Longing for us to fall into His arms and rest.

> We are not victims; we are God's daughters. And He has not left us on our own.

To stop running. Stop hiding.

To be still . . . cease striving . . . and know that He is God (Psalm 46:10 NIV; NASB). He is our Healer. Redeemer. And Re-Creator.

He makes all things new—and that includes you and me!

One Radical Woman

It all happened so fast. She felt confused. Men were yelling, grabbing her arms. Dragging her out of the house. Shouting. Cursing. Calling her names.

Whore. Slut. Worthless. No-good. Lowlife.

It cut through her like a knife.

The men whispered among themselves. She couldn't make out much but heard something about a test. A test for some popular religious leader? She cringed inside.

She heard the men sneering about what the Rabbi would do with her. Their words were punctuated by coarse laughter as they anticipated His response.

It would be death. Certain death.

Heart pounding. Body frozen in dread. Fear's cold fingers worked their way up her spine. She winced. Her body could feel the stones that were waiting to be thrown at her. She imagined the jeering crowds, celebrating justice.

But justice would be her destruction.

Another man spat on her, saying whores like her would burn in hell.

These religious leaders had burst in on her in the middle of a sexual encounter. Caught in the act. Her lover fled, leaving her to fend for herself. The romance was shattered. The moment destroyed.

What happened? Was it a scheme? A trick? Have I been duped?

Her lover . . . he had seemed so gentle, so caring. But no, he had abandoned her. Left her with these cruel, ruthless men.

She hung her head. *Maybe they're right. I do deserve to die.*

Her bare feet were bruised and bleeding from trying to keep up. The religious leaders surrounded her on all sides. There was no escape. This was her fate. A victim of some sick plot.

And then she saw Him. The Rabbi. He was surrounded by a crowd of people. Her neighbors. Friends.

Shame swept over her like a tidal wave. No one knew the full story. No one understood.

The religious leaders began listing out her offenses to the Rabbi. It seemed like they were enjoying it too. "This woman was caught red-handed in the act of adultery. Moses, in the Law, gives orders to stone such persons. What do you say?"

She felt like her heart was being torn out. No hope now. Her breath stuck in her throat, waiting. Waiting for the Rabbi's death sentence. She dared not even look His way.

But He caught her eye. One glimpse . . . and her fear melted away as quickly as it had come. He knew. Somehow, in some way, He knew her story. He knew *her*. He saw her desperate heart.

And in His eyes, she saw pure love. Compassion. Not a hint of judgment or anger.

> In His eyes, she saw pure love. Compassion. Not a hint of judgment or anger.

What do You say? What do You say? The men's words rang in her ears.

The Rabbi didn't answer. It almost seemed like He ignored them. Bending down, He wrote something in the dirt.

She couldn't make out the letters, but her capturers were surprised. Angry. Aghast.

"The sinless one among you, go first: Throw the stone." Jesus' words were perplexing. What did He mean?

The religious leaders stopped firing questions. Stepped back. Let go of her wrists. Walked away. Silence fell on the crowd.

She rubbed her bruised wrists, trying to make sense of it all.

The Rabbi stood up. Walked toward her. *Is He going to stone me Himself?*

Shame and guilt surged back. He was a good man—a holy man. And she? She was nothing. *Whore. Slut. Worthless. Lowlife.*

"Where are they?" His voice was tender. Firm. Reassuring. He was talking to her.

Her words stuck in her throat. Men didn't talk to women, particularly a woman in her position.

"Does no one condemn you?" He asked her, compassion spilling over.

"No one, Master," she whispered.

"Neither do I," He said. "Go on your way. From now on, don't sin."

She couldn't believe His words. Her feet were glued to the ground. Her heart pounded in her chest—only this time, not out of fear. Out of shock. Surprise. Sheer joy.

Go? He's going to let me go? Why . . . how?

Seconds ago, she had stared death in the face, and now . . . this unexpected grace and forgiveness?

I wonder what burst out of her heart in response to Jesus' tender confrontation. I wonder what else Jesus said to her that day before they parted ways.

Regardless of their exact exchange, one thing is clear: she was a changed woman.

She rebelled.

She rebelled against the lies that said she was a worthless, no-good slut. She rebelled against the religious leaders who told her she'd burn in hell. She rebelled against it all and listened to the clear words of Jesus.

No more shame. No more guilt. No more running or hiding or covering up. No more escapades in the dark. It seemed cheap and shallow in comparison with this sheer love.

No more, she vowed. *No more will I live as a victim. I am more. Created for more. I will not cheapen myself again.*

Forgiven. Rescued. Redeemed.

And that can be our story too. The same Rabbi who reached out and offered hope to this Jewish woman also reaches out to you and me. Offering grace. Forgiveness. Mercy. Healing. A second (and third . . . and hundredth) chance.[17]

Will you listen to His words? Let them seep down into your bruised and broken heart? He will meet you there.

I beg you, don't turn away.

What's Your Story?

Everybody has a story. And those pictures, memories, and voices from the past have great power to shape us—either to destroy us or to help us discover our life mission and purpose. Maybe you can relate to the experiences of Rachel, Felicia, or Brandi.

"I struggle with depression and negative self-image," Rachel admitted. "When I was fourteen, I was gang-raped by my boyfriend and several other guys. Even now, ten years later, I still have visible scars on my body. Most likely, I will never be able to have children. Some days I feel used, ugly, and worthless. Sometimes I wonder if God even loves me anymore."

Felicia's story is no less tragic. "My twin brother was my best friend growing up. When he was killed in a school shooting, I became angry . . . then anxious. Always looking over my shoulder wondering, *Will I be next?* I even contemplated taking my own life, thinking it might be better to die than live without him. I started to lose hope. It hurt so bad and I didn't know how I would go on."

"My boyfriend and I started messing around with sex, and he said that if I really loved him I'd give it to him," Brandi said. "Of course I loved him! So I did. I was shocked and horrified to be staring at a positive pregnancy test a few weeks later. My parents hated my boyfriend and certainly wouldn't approve. So I didn't tell anyone. I 'took care of it,' as the doctor said. But my soul aches, and sometimes I wonder, *How could I kill my own child?*"

What's your story? Your secret? Your bondage?

Even ten or twenty years later . . . we remember the moment, the ache, the shame. It can be crippling. It can suck the life out of us. But it doesn't have to.

I say it's time to rebel against the idea that these moments dictate our life or our future. To rebel against the victim mentality. To dare to believe that we break through and experience freedom from our pasts. That rather than running and hiding, our stories of shame can become testimonies of hope. Redemption. Change.

Tim Keller wisely writes, "If you want God's grace, all you need is need, all you need is nothing."[18] It's not a matter of getting your act together or saving yourself. That's God's deal. All we have to do is come.

Rachel is more than a rape victim. She shared, "I'm God's daughter. His precious daughter. I don't know why He allowed this to happen to me, but I am a fighter. I won't let this rob me of my future. As I am beginning to heal, I want to help other women who have been raped not to live as victims."

Felicia is more than a survivor. "God has not left me on my own. My pity party was really my choice . . . and I don't want to waste my life with regrets and what-ifs. It was out of my control—as much as I loved my twin brother, I couldn't protect him. But I can live in a way that honors his death. I can help other people who face tragedy to cling on to hope."

Brandi is more than a woman who had an abortion. "I can't undo what I did, but I'm wrestling to accept and live in God's forgiveness. There is no condemnation in Him, and I cling to that whenever the gruesome memories haunt me. When guilt and shame drown out His truth, I reach out to a friend for help and support. I want to be there for other women, too, so we can heal together . . . and help our friends choose life."

These three women are courageously rebelling. Rebelling against the pathway of brokenness and chaos. Rebelling against the thought, *God's not there for me.* Rebelling against our culture's lie of "fake it until you make it."

They are vulnerable. Honest. God-confident. They are heroes. Far from empty shells of who they once were, they are being transformed . . . and God is using them to help other women break free too.

Nobody's perfect. I have my own share of hurts and struggles. Battling cystic acne as a teenager left its mark on my identity long after the pockmarks faded. Some days, I don't even want to look in the mirror. Self-loathing and negativity creep in, and I'm ready to scream if I see one more Photoshopped advertisement of a "perfect" woman. Isn't it weird how something you know is fake can still bring up insecurity? I've had to wrestle through the true meaning of beauty and how my external appearance fits into that. It's so easy to become a slave to appearance and to lose sight of what really matters.

In the midst of it all, the glorious truth is that our issues, brokenness, and struggles don't have to define us.

I want to rebel. I want to rebel against my past circumstances and voices that tell me who I am or how I will live my life. It's a tragedy that so many women live as victims when there is a way out!

I also want to rebel against the lies of church culture. One of those is that brokenness is unacceptable . . . shameful . . . dirty . . . wrong. *Once you know Christ, all your troubles will magically disappear, right?* I hate to break it to you, but that's not true. Yes, He is kind. He is merciful. But sometimes, He gives us the strength to get through our pain instead of removing it.

God doesn't promise us a pain-free, easy life, but He offers us Himself. Pain is a gift to us, and hardship shapes us . . . if we let it.

So don't buy the lie of "having it all together"—every hair in place and the perfect designer bag to match our shoes. Being well-kempt may hide the pain from outsiders, but it doesn't heal the aching wounds in our souls.

> The beauty is that in those broken places, God will meet us. He has not left us alone.

Messiness. Brokenness. Pain. We can't cover it up. Can't hide it. Can't heal ourselves. Yet the beauty is that in those broken places, God will meet us. He has not left us alone.

Driven to the Heart of God

I've seen firsthand how one of the most powerful tools God uses in our healing journey is a safe community of other women. Women we trust . . . women we can pour out our hearts to—the good, the bad, and the ugly—and know they are there for us to support and love us through it all. To speak truth. To cry with us. To rebel with us.

Over the years, I've had the privilege of meeting and hearing the stories of brave young women who have reached out in the midst of great pain. Women struggling with depression, eating disorders, panic attacks, addictions, and past abuse. And I've been amazed at how helpful professional counseling can be. Meeting with a Christian counselor doesn't mean you're sick, weird, or totally messed up. It just means you're human—and that you're taking the initiative to step out of that victim mode and into freedom.

You don't have to suffer alone. The most courageous women are those who are willing to step out. To tell their story and break out of bondage.

God says to us, "Strength! Courage! Don't be timid; don't get discouraged. GOD, your God, is with you every step you take" (Joshua 1:9). He will not leave us to take these painful steps toward healing without Him.

With new strength and a new vision, we can learn to live in a radically different way. Forget trying to compensate for past mistakes. Cover up guilt. Or perform for others.

If you think admitting your struggles is hard, believe me . . . I'm right there with you. I'm a

> With new strength and a new vision, we can learn to live in a radically different way.

perfectionist by nature. I want to make straight As in class, excel at my job, love Ben well, and have strong, meaningful relationships. That's a lot to juggle—and sometimes, when I feel overwhelmed, the controlling side of me rears its ugly head. Let me tell you, it ain't pretty! It's uncomfortable and downright embarrassing to admit that I don't have it all together. That I need help and support from others. And that some days, I need to cut myself some slack. Rather than beating myself up, I need to revel in God's grace and unconditional love, even—and perhaps especially—in the midst of my failures. I'll be honest, it's a hard pill for a girl like me to swallow, but I'm learning to accept my limitations as gifts that remind me of my need for God—and loving, supportive friends.

So you're not perfect—so what? None of us is. But Jesus didn't come to save perfect people; He came to rescue, heal, and restore broken people. Take a look at the Gospel of Matthew. Jesus said, "Who needs a doctor: the healthy or the sick? Go figure out what this Scripture means: 'I'm after mercy, not religion'" (Matthew 9:12). He never meant for us to attain perfection on this earth. Instead, He longs for us to see His grace and mercy through our imperfections.

Brennan Manning wrote a book called *The Ragamuffin Gospel: Good News for the Bedraggled, Beat-Up, and Burnt Out.* I love what he says: "For those who feel their lives are a grave disappointment to God, it requires enormous trust and reckless, raging confidence to accept that the love of Christ knows no shadow of alteration or change."[19]

No shadow of alteration or change. That's how God loves us.

Manning goes on to point out the gift of brokenness: "For Ragamuffins, God's name is Mercy. We see our darkness as a prized possession because it drives us into the heart of God. Without mercy our darkness would plunge us into despair—and for some, self-destruction."[20]

Will you let your own personal "darkness" drive you to the heart of God?

> Will you let your own personal "darkness" drive you to the heart of God?

If God, the One ultimately offended by sin, can forgive us . . . why is it so hard to forgive ourselves? It's so easy to let our past define where we'll go in the future. It's even harder when we blame ourselves for things we had no control over.

You may say, "I'm no longer a virgin" or "I was sexually abused," and believe that you're damaged goods . . . that you will never deserve the love of God or a good man. Maybe you hate yourself because of a past abortion. Or maybe you're angry at God because a friend committed suicide or was killed in a car accident.

I don't know your specific situation, but I do know this: God will not abandon you. He will not leave you on your own. "Don't despair. Your GOD is present among you, a strong Warrior there to save you. Happy to have you back, he'll calm you with his love and delight you with his songs" (Zephaniah 3:16–17).

Let Down Your Walls

"Are you tired?" Jesus lovingly asks. "Worn out? . . . Come to me. Get away with me and you'll recover your life. I'll show you how to take a real rest" (Matthew 11:28).

This is the way out.

If we dare to let go. To rebel against our fear of stereotypes. Judgment. Criticism. To see through the lie that God could never forgive us.

> Jesus tells us to come to Him with our pain and find rest in Him.

He doesn't say, "I don't want to see your mess; keep it to yourself. Pull your act together."

Far from it! He says, "Come to Me." He welcomes us to come, just as we are. With the guilt of an abortion. With the scars of abuse. With bitterness toward an absent father. Or anger toward a guy who took advantage of us and then walked out.

God is pure love. He is safe. He is trustworthy. He is our way out. Through Him, we can learn to release the pain we've kept buried inside and find new hope.

"Nobody escapes being wounded," Henri Nouwen points out. "We all are wounded people, whether physically, emotionally, mentally, or spiritually. The main question is not 'How can we hide our wounds?' so we don't have to be embarrassed, but 'How can we put our woundedness in the service of others?' When our wounds cease to be a source of shame, and become a source of healing, we have become wounded healers."[21]

Healing will come. I love this promise from Malachi. It is God's promise for us, His daughters . . . *no matter what we've experienced.* "But for you, sunrise! The sun of righteousness will dawn on those who honor my name, healing radiating from its wings" (Malachi 4:2).

Healing radiating from its wings. What a beautiful picture. The psalmist even says, "His huge outstretched arms protect you—under them you're perfectly safe; his arms fend off all harm" (Psalm 91:4).

We can rest safely in His arms.

My dad often says that brokenness begs for healing, that wherever there is pain, our Father God longs to come in and make whole. As we go along, perhaps we'll find that it's our weaknesses and failures that He uses the most to show His power and redeeming love. I've certainly found this to be true in my own life. Even though I have to still often fight a battle with insecurity and perfectionism, God is setting me free from the lies that once controlled me. It's not that we'll never struggle again, but God's healing power can transform a gaping wound into a scar of remembrance. Scars that tell a story of God's grace, mercy, and redemption.

> God's healing power can transform a gaping wound into a scar of remembrance. Scars that tell a story of God's grace, mercy, and redemption.

"No wound heals quickly," Mo Isom points out. "But given time, and care and patience, those wounds scab again and eventually scar. . . . A reminder of the pain we endured. A reminder of the lessons we learned."[22]

I love the song "Pieces" by Red.[23] If you haven't listened to it before, stop and YouTube it! As women, we often try so hard, but we can't fix ourselves. We can't run. We can't hide.

The only real answer is to come to Jesus. In pieces—broken, scarred, maybe even shattered. He is the only One who has the freedom and power to make us whole.

Wholeness. Freedom. That's what I want. Not self-pity, fear, and shame.

God alone has the power to draw us out of the darkness and into His marvelous light. So let's not waste any time. Let's stretch out our hands and grab hold of His grace.

Let's join Mo—no longer living as victims of an eating disorder. Depression. An absent father. Drugs. Past abuse. Perfectionism. Insecurity. Or anything else.

We were created to be Spirit-filled, fearless, free daughters of God. Not defined by our past but by the One we follow.

What are we waiting for? Let's dare to rebel—today and every day—and live free.

CHAPTER FOUR

Dare to Believe

I believe in Christ like I believe in
the sun, not just because I see it, but
because by it I can see everything else.

—*C. S. Lewis*

Growing up, I made very few "forever" friends. Jen has been one of those friends to me. Funny. Encouraging. Kind. Humble. Beautiful. Bright.

I always knew Jen had my back. We shared a lot of secrets, a lot of tears, and a lot of schemes to prank our brothers.

Jen was my shopping buddy, my study partner, and my best friend. But more than anything, I loved Jen because she was passionate about sharing the love of Jesus.

Whether at a Junior Miss pageant or gymnastics competition, Jen would always mention something about Jesus: "God alone is the only One worth living for," I remember her telling the crowd at Cheer Nationals. "God has always been there for me, and He is my confidence and strength when I am weak. I want to use all my talents and abilities to serve Him."

I still remember being giddy with excitement when we both were accepted into our high school's concert choir.

Our first performance was November 5, 2006. I took my place with pride next to Jen and squeezed her hand. Who cared that we were a little off key? As we sang the words of "Lord, You're Holy," I couldn't have dreamed how our lives were about to change. Forever.

A drunk driver. Eighty miles an hour. A curve on a dark road.

Jen's family was hit head-on as they were driving home from church that night. All four family members were airlifted to ICU units.

Dad didn't know how to break the news to me: My best friend in the whole world had suffered multiple skull fractures. Severe brain trauma. She probably wouldn't survive the night.

It hit me like a ton of bricks. I collapsed in my dad's arms as tears rolled down my face.

Where are You, God?

How could You let this happen . . . to Jen, of all people? She loves You.

I wanted to scream in protest. Just a few hours earlier, Jen and I had been singing our hearts out, lifting our hands in praise. Now I wanted to shake my fist at God.

What's crazy is that Jen had been praying for God to work in her life. I remember catching each other many mornings before school and spending a few moments talking to God: "Do something big through me, Jesus." Jen's prayers were always so sincere. "Use me in a special way for Your glory . . . to point other people to You."

I tried unsuccessfully to push these words out of my mind as I stood over the hospital bed. I barely recognized my friend. Jen was connected to tubes, monitors, IVs. Large bandages hid cuts, bruises, and wounds.

I wanted to hug her. To hold her. Tell her everything was going to be okay.

But I couldn't. I was completely powerless. It's a terrifying feeling to watch your friend suffer and be helpless to do anything.

You crushed one of my best friends. How dare You, God! How could You do that?

The tears started to fall again, but I tried to be strong. And pray. Even in the midst of my anger at God, I begged Him to save Jen's life. To heal her.

Nothing happened . . . no booming voice from heaven. No lightning from the sky.

Jen lingered in a coma. She was barely clinging to life. Day. After day. After day. The doctors weren't sure if she'd ever wake up, and they warned that if she did, she would be screaming and cursing in confusion because of her severe brain injuries.

The clock moved in slow motion. I dragged myself out of bed every day. Waiting. Hoping. Praying for a miracle.

Five weeks passed. And Jen opened her eyes. But rather than cursing, she began singing. Praying. Reciting God's promises.

What's crazy is that Jen didn't even know who she was. Where she was. Who her parents were. Who I was. She didn't know how to brush her teeth or what to do with a shoe. She didn't know that two plus two equals four or that she had a brother.

But one thing she did remember: Jesus.

Despite her severe brain injuries, Jen remembered a lot of the worship songs we'd sung in choir together. The scriptures we'd memorized together as little girls.

"The Holy Spirit shone clear and brilliant in her and through her," Jen's mom, Linda, remembers.[1]

In the midst of unspeakable tragedy, Jen still dared to believe. She was angry, and it was hard for her to forgive the man who had caused the wreck. But she chose to believe that God has a purpose and plan for everything.[2]

We all prayed and hoped and waited for God to heal Jen—to make her the way she was before the accident.

But it didn't happen that way. Seven years later, Jen still suffers from her brain injuries, including cortical blindness and short-term memory loss. She faces pain every single day. As I'm writing this, Jen has just found out she has thyroid cancer.

For a long time, I prayed that God would restore Jen's physical health. I doubted. I struggled. I questioned God. My faith was so weak.

Looking back now, I see that His plans are far better than mine. God is making my beautiful friend Jen extraordinary. Jen is living above her circumstances. Beyond her own strength. Her faith always challenges me.

"God has been with me . . . every step of the way, and He still is carrying me," Jen says. "One day at a time . . . I just have to be constantly reminding myself that His plan is perfect."[3]

God is using Jen's story to bring other people to Him from all around the world. Jen still has scars from the accident, but she looks at them in a new light. "Jesus has scars too," she tells audiences when she speaks. "His scars shout, 'I love you,' 'You were worth it,' and 'I don't regret what I did for you.'"

Jen dares to believe.

To believe that in the midst of a shattered life God can work a miracle. Far greater than her physical healing, that miracle is other people's lives being changed.

This courageous woman chooses to see God's faithfulness— His redemption in the midst of her pain.

"I love how God takes all of our scars and turns them into beauty marks for his glory!" Jen posted on Facebook recently.

Every single day, my friend rebels against hopelessness. The victim mind-set. The lies that if God loved her, life would be easy.

Jen's body is broken and scarred—and now she is fighting cancer—but her heart is flourishing.

She is vibrant. Alive. Free.

Surrender in a DIY World

"I believe in God, but . . ." If you search the phrase on Google, you'll find more than three hundred million results.

"I believe in God, but I don't trust Him with my life. I want my own way. I want to be happy. I want to be in control. I don't trust Him with my future husband. My career. My friendships." And on it goes.

This is the cultural Kool-Aid we've drunk, and it's killing us spiritually. It's weak. Feeble. Based on circumstances. It doesn't hold up in crisis. It's a pack of lies.

Our culture tells us the only person you can really trust is yourself. Do it yourself. *Pull yourself up by your own bootstraps. If there is a God, He's probably busy with bigger problems than yours.* We may not actually say that, but often we live like it.

> Many times, we shut God out. We miss out on real, raw faith.

And so we try to control. Manipulate. Rescue ourselves. Hide the pain. And many times, we shut God out. We miss out on real, raw faith.

I've had the opportunity to meet many Christian women all across the country through my mom's ministry, Extraordinary Women.[4] And there seems to be several extremes. Perhaps you can identify with me.

The church lady. She's the pious, religious woman who looks like she has it all together but is dying inside. She makes a show of religion and uses Christian talk to make herself seem important. To impress others. To look good. I like to call it the glitzy version of Christianity. It's "having a form of godliness but denying its power" (2 Timothy 3:5 NIV). Does she really know Jesus? Sometimes I wonder, particularly when I see how she treats others. Gossiping, backbiting, destroying anyone who gets in her way.

"Surrender?" She pauses. "Why would I? I've got my life under control."

The double agent. She's in the front row at church every Sunday, raising her hands . . . seemingly lost in worship. But if you ran into her on Friday or Saturday night, you'd find quite a different story. Partying. Sleeping around. Desperate for someone—anyone—to notice her. To love her, or at least "use" her, so she won't have to spend the night alone. Is she following Jesus? She's more consumed with the hot guy in the room.

"Surrender?" She laughs. "Maybe later . . . but certainly not now."

The wounded woman. She's been dealt a bad hand in life. Maybe her dad walked out. Her friend committed suicide. Her husband cheated on her. This woman pastes on a brave smile, but inside she's losing hope. Questions like "How could God love me if . . . ?" and "Why would God allow . . . ?" plague her mind and heart. What she knows about God is a far cry from what she's feeling in the moment.

"Surrender?" she whispers. "How can I when I don't trust Him?"

Three women—all trying to find faith, but none of them willing to trust. There's something missing in today's version of Christianity.

Many churches are dying—closing their doors. More millennials than ever are leaving organized religion. There is a 43 percent drop-off in church engagement among teenagers and twenty-somethings.[5]

Research suggests that 50 percent of eighteen- to twenty-nine-year-olds are frustrated by faith, and nearly 40 percent wrestle with significant doubt.[6]

Why? Because we've bought a false, shallow faith. A faith that says, "When I'm happy and life is going the way I want, I'll love God—but when He tries to mess with my plans, it ain't gonna end up pretty. God must not love me if He doesn't give me what I want."

Spirituality today is like the classic all-American buffet. Pick and choose what sounds appetizing (and make sure to load up on dessert!), but pass by the brussels sprouts and broccoli, so to speak.

Pick a God who loves you and has a wonderful plan for your life, but pass by verses like "In this world you will have trouble" (John 16:33 NIV).

Load up on promises of blessing and prosperity, but disregard truths like, "Don't run from suffering; embrace it. Follow me and I'll show you how. . . . Self-sacrifice is the way, my way, to finding yourself, your true self" (Matthew 16:24).

Add an extra serving of God's mercy, acceptance, and forgiveness, but ignore Jesus' words that make us squirm: "What is required is serious obedience—*doing* what my Father wills" (Matthew 7:21).

Cheap grace. That's what German pastor and martyr Dietrich Bonhoeffer called it: "The preaching of forgiveness without requiring repentance, baptism without church discipline, Communion without confession . . . grace without discipleship, grace without the cross, grace without Jesus Christ, living and incarnate."[7]

When tragedy hits, like it did for Jen, cheap grace quickly crumbles. It doesn't hold water. It doesn't answer our deep questions or help us make sense of life's problems and hardships.

> When tragedy hits . . . cheap grace quickly crumbles.

One Radical Woman

Laughter. Little hands reaching out to her. Slobbery kisses. A baby to cuddle. As Hannah rubbed her sleepy eyes, she realized it was just another dream.

She ached to think of it. As she dragged herself out of bed, the familiar wave of sadness swept over her again. Deafening silence. Empty arms.

Tears welled up in her eyes.

Why, God? What have I done to deserve this? She'd asked the same questions a thousand times.

But there were no answers. Just the noise of the neighborhood children clamoring for breakfast. The prods of other women who would ask about her and Elkanah, offering various things they thought might help with her childlessness. But underneath the concern was scorn. Judgment. The words mocked her.

One year passed after their wedding day, and her friends told her to just give it some time.

Two years, and she began to worry.

Five years, and most of the women she knew had their hands full. They complained, but she'd give anything to have a baby. *Who cares about colic, dirty diapers, and sleepless nights?*

Friends started to rub it in, pointing out that if God really loved her, He would give her a child.

Her husband told her to get over it. "Am I not of more worth to you than ten sons?"

Even church had become a place of judgment: "Every time she went to the sanctuary of GOD she could expect to be taunted."

Hannah eventually stopped dreaming. Now she lay awake at night, tormented by their words.

God, I haven't asked for a lot—I didn't ask for a fancy house or a huge inheritance. All I ever wanted was to be a mother. Why are You so cruel? Where are You? Do You even care?

No one understood. No one. Even God was silent.

Many years, and she had all but given up hope. Depression and despair consumed her. She had to force herself to get out of bed. To eat.

Give up . . . stop believing. Trusting. Waiting. Praying. God has forgotten you.

The pain of those words pierced her heart. Could it be true?

She fought to hang on to that glimmer of hope that God was with her. And with her last ounce of strength, she ran to Him.

Heartbroken. Defeated. Resentful. Desperate.

The tears flowed as she poured out her heart. Holding nothing back.

"Oh, GOD-of-the-Angel-Armies . . . take a good, hard look at my pain," she begged. "Quit neglecting me and go into action for me."

As time dragged by and Hannah continued praying silently, Eli the priest began to wonder about her. *What's up with this woman? Is she drunk?*

"The only thing I've been pouring out is my heart, pouring it out to GOD," Hannah told him. "It's because I'm so desperately unhappy and in such pain that I've stayed here so long."

Even the priest didn't really understand. Yet she stayed. Stayed in God's presence because He was her only hope.

How easy it would have been to become bitter. To curse God and turn away. To shake her hand in His face.

But no, she cried out to God in the midst of her deepest pain and confusion. *I know that God is good. Sovereign. Loving. He cannot forget His children.*

> Hannah dared to believe. She saw the miracle before it happened.

With that realization, Hannah dared to believe. She saw the miracle before it happened. And in her confidence that God would come through by giving her a son, she made a vow: "I'll give him completely, unreservedly to you. I'll set him apart for a life of holy discipline."

And her answer came unexpectedly.

"Go in peace," Eli said. "And may the God of Israel give you what you have asked of him."

There were no lightning bolts. No handwriting on the wall. Only the voice of a faithful priest. But Hannah saw it was a message from God Himself. *It will happen!* she thought. *God does not lie.*

Peace spread through her weary body. Hope revived her aching heart. Her face was radiant with confidence in God.

Hannah was "fully convinced that God was able to do what he had promised" (Romans 4:21 ESV).

She relaxed. Enjoyed a good dinner. Slept deeply. Woke up early and worshipped God for the gift she hadn't yet received.

Hannah rebelled against all the lies. The taunts of her friends. The apathy of her husband.

She dared to believe. And God was true to His word. Months later, as she held her baby boy, Samuel, she remembered her vow—to give her son to God.

I wonder if Hannah battled with herself as she nursed baby Samuel. *Surely God will understand how much I love my son . . . I mean, I made that vow in a moment of panic—I wasn't in my right mind. How could God take away something so precious? Something I've spent my life waiting and praying for?*

But for Hannah, it was a matter of obedience. As soon as Samuel was weaned, she took the bittersweet journey toward the temple. The memories flooded back: her despair . . . God's faithfulness . . . and now little Samuel as proof.

She looked over him and smiled, desperately trying to swallow the lump in her throat. Everything in her screamed, *No! Don't do it! Are you crazy?*

God is good, she reminded herself, *and I will trust Him, even when it hurts.*

> God is good . . . and I will trust Him, even when it hurts.

"Would you believe that I'm the very woman who was standing before you at this very spot, praying to GOD?" she asked Eli the priest. "I prayed for this child, and GOD gave me what I asked for. And now I have dedicated him to GOD. He's dedicated to GOD for life."

There, it was done. And even as the tears stung her eyes, she broke into praise:

> GOD knows what's going on.
>> He takes the measure of everything that happens. . . .
>> The weak are infused with fresh strength. . . .
>> The hungry are getting second helpings. . . .
> GOD brings death and GOD brings life. . . .
>> He lowers, he also lifts up. . . .
>> He rekindles burned-out lives with fresh hope. . . .
> He protectively cares for his faithful friends, step by step. . . .
> GOD will set things right all over the earth.

Because one radical woman dared to believe—against all hope—God raised up Hannah's son, Samuel, to be a prophet and judge who would change the course of history and pave the way for Jesus Christ.

I wonder how the story might have ended if Hannah had given up hope. What if she'd said, like we so often do, "But I just don't feel God! He's not coming through for me . . . If God loves me, why isn't He making it all better?"

In Hannah's case—and often in our lives too—God doesn't provide quick, easy, and painless answers. Maybe you've been tempted to give God the finger and tell Him to get lost. Maybe you've run as far from God as you possibly can. Or maybe you're a doubter, like me.

Hannah's words echo down through history, tearing at our independence: "No one makes it in this life by sheer muscle!" Instead, God "rekindles burned-out lives with fresh hope."[8]

How might our stories be different if we dare to believe?

Are You Willing to Fight?

I battle often to trust God. To believe that He is going to show up in my life. It's so easy to want to take back control. As a recovering perfectionist, I can easily feel that any sign of weakness or failure will lead to rejection. So if I don't perform at 100 percent, I can wrestle with insecurity, guilt, and self-loathing. And it's deadly for my soul.

I need wisdom from God's Word and the Holy Spirit to help me see the truth that His love for me is absolutely unconditional and unchanging. I need to remind my wayward heart of God's promises and His faithfulness toward me—even in my weakest moments.

It's hard sometimes because we can't see God. There's a tendency to think that maybe God is good, but He isn't necessarily good toward me, especially when life doesn't make sense. But a relationship with Him is the only way to counter these negative, condemning thoughts. And that's where faith comes in. Romans 4:20–21 (ESV) are my "fight" verses that I come back to often. I personalize them to my life: "No unbelief will make me waver concerning the promise of God. I will grow strong in my faith as I give glory to God, fully convinced that God is able to do what He has promised."

> To survive spiritually in this world, we need to preach the gospel to ourselves . . . every single day.

To survive spiritually in this world, we need to preach the gospel to ourselves . . . every single day. I don't know about you, but I need new faith to believe that God hasn't given up on me. That it's not up to me to fix myself, but that God is at work transforming and growing me, if I have a willing heart.

Believing God starts with rebelling against the whole pack of lies. Ignoring the taunts and judgment of others. And like Hannah, running into His presence. Throwing ourselves at His feet. Crying out to Him as our only hope.

Taking the risk to be gut honest. Bringing Him our resentment, anger, desperation, and pain. Facing our doubts and questions. Fighting to believe that He is with us and *for* us.

And here's what's amazing: God already knows the pain that's in our hearts. He sees the wounds. The guilt. The regret. There are no secrets from Him. Yet He loves us . . . with an unchanging, life-giving, radical love.

This love has power to change everything. The Bible says, "He heals the heartbroken and bandages their wounds" (Psalm 147:3).

Emotional wounds are no less traumatizing or painful than a broken bone. Both have the power to permanently scar and cripple us if we ignore them. Denying pain doesn't make it go away. It just festers.

But there is hope. "I call to God," the psalmist writes. "GOD will help me. At dusk, dawn, and noon I sigh deep sighs—he hears, he rescues" (Psalm 55:16–17).

He hears. He rescues.

From Feeling to Following

We want Jesus. How do I know? Despite leaving churches, nearly half of young people ages eighteen to twenty-nine say they want "a more traditional faith, rather than a hip version of Christianity."[9]

We've got to go back to our roots. Christianity isn't a menu to pick and choose from. It's not a Sunday service, and it's not about a nice dress, a fake smile, and a big study Bible.

Following Jesus is a lifestyle of surrender. Trust. Bold faith. Dying to

> Following Jesus is a lifestyle of surrender.

what we want. Clinging to Jesus when the world seems to be in chaos around us.

Allowing Him to transform the way we act, think, and feel rather than clinging tightly to control of our lives.

Choosing to live in dependence on Him rather than independent of Him.

This is costly grace. To dare to believe God and follow Him, even when it's not popular, fun, or easy. Even when it doesn't make sense. Even when we feel alone in a crowd.

Bonhoeffer writes, "Such grace is *costly* because it calls us to follow . . . Jesus Christ. It is costly because it costs a man his life, and it is grace because it gives a man the only true life. It is costly because it condemns sin, and grace because it justifies the sinner. Above all it is *costly* because it cost God the life of his Son . . . and what has cost God much cannot be cheap for us."[10]

I wrestle often with the idea that if Jesus is who He says He is, then He's everything. That should really define us. His life, His ways, His heart. But so often it doesn't.

Jen Barrick's life challenges and convicts me. All she really has is her relationship with Jesus and her family . . . and I'm learning it's all she really needs. Sure, there are still unanswered questions. Disappointments. Pain. Daily challenges. And now, cancer.[11]

But there is an unashamed God-beauty in Jen, and it challenges me to know Him and press into Him more.

I want to believe God. To trust Him fully. To follow Him radically. To know that He is the only One who can meet the deepest longings of my heart.

It's hard to surrender like that. It goes against the grain of everything we've been taught about independence. Individuality. Getting our way.

But I want to rebel against everything that pulls me away from intimacy with God.

Rebel against the idea that it's wrong to have doubts. To wrestle with God. To beg Him for answers. To bring our anger and pain to Him.

Rebel against our natural tendency to try to figure out life on our own rather than seeking God and wrestling with Him.

Rebel against the halfhearted faith that defines modern-day Christianity—that says you can trust Him for salvation but not everyday life.

Rebel against this false idea of an absent God who doesn't care about us and isn't there.

God is looking for women whose faith is radical.

Women who will be rebellious—and live free.

God's Word tells us, "The eyes of the Lord range throughout the earth to strengthen those whose hearts are fully committed to him" (2 Chronicles 16:9 NIV).

Fully committed. All in. Undivided.

I want to be that kind of woman.

CHAPTER FIVE

I Am Woman

> The fact that I am a woman does not
> make me a different kind of Christian,
> but the fact that I am a Christian does
> make me a different kind of woman.
>
> —*Elisabeth Elliot*

GLITZ. GLAMOUR. MILLIONS LOOKING ON. It's one of the world's brightest stages. Evening gown. Swimsuit competition. A public platform to advocate for.

Ultimately, fighting for the coveted crown.

It's the Miss America pageant, a US tradition for nearly one hundred years. Hosted by some of the world's biggest stars. Judges evaluate and rate contestants based on talent, poise, confidence, fitness, and more.

Enter Teresa Scanlan. One of seven kids. Homeschooled. Growing up in small-town Nebraska.

As a little girl, Teresa had a warm smile. Blonde curls. A sparkle in her eyes. And a love for Jesus.

Yet she was painfully shy. Sensitive. Hard on herself. Uncomfortable around others. And quirky too. In fact, Teresa loved to make her own clothes out of duct tape.

A duct-tape dress? Not exactly the makings of Miss America. Or was it?

As Teresa explored the world of pageants, she became painfully aware of the pressure toward perfection. Extreme diets. Borderline starvation. Unhealthy exercise plans. It was all about "fake" beauty.

And this brave young woman refused to buy in.

Thirteen-year-old Teresa promised herself that she wouldn't damage her body in order to gain success at pageants. Fighting to accept herself in a world where physical appearance is everything, Teresa faced some tough decisions.

Yet rather than dismiss the pageant world altogether, Teresa claimed it as an opportunity for godly influence. To make a difference . . . even as a teenager.

Teresa chose to make her Miss America campaign about eating disorders, in a world where dress size and physical beauty reign.

She chose to speak out about the pressures society puts on us. To take a stand against society's unrealistic standards of beauty and challenge women to accept and be confident in who God created them to be.

But that didn't mean looking ugly or homely. Teresa intentionally cultivated her physical beauty, but in a healthy, nondestructive way.

Teresa prepared for the pageant, but she didn't go to extremes. She once joked to a reporter that she didn't give up cookies for the event.[1]

Nails, makeup, fashion. When her hair was severely damaged, Teresa even chose to be fitted for a wig.

But even as she prepared outwardly, she also cultivated the beauty of her heart. A deep love for people. A desire to speak out to offer hope. Time and again, she was forced to trust God and lay down control. She couldn't control the outcome.

Teresa was fearless. She often fell back on God's promises when insecurity reared its ugly head: "This I know, that God is for me. . . . In God I trust; I shall not be afraid. What can man do to me?" (Psalm 56:9, 11 ESV).

January 5, 2011. The pressure was on.

A long way from her small hometown, seventeen-year-old Teresa took the stage in front of thousands at the Planet Hollywood Resort and Casino in Las Vegas. Nearly seven million were watching around the world.

Way out of my league. Too young. Too inexperienced. Too immature.

But Teresa fought back against those negative thoughts. She knew God had placed her in the Miss America competition for a reason. And no matter what the outcome of the pageant, she was determined to show God's love on and off the stage.[2]

Teresa got it. She saw through the glitz and glamour to the heart of her purpose as a woman—to use her influence and platform to break down the lies of culture and share the love of Christ.

The final competition. Rather than primping, worrying, or talking with friends, Teresa slipped away to spend some time in prayer before she walked onstage.

I can't imagine the torture of waiting. The pressure. The hype. The stress. Yet as she held her breath for the final pronouncement, Teresa clung to her true identity.

"Ladies and gentlemen, your Miss America 2011 is . . . *Miss Nebraska!*"

Teresa was in shock. Trying to hold back the tears, she raised both hands high as the crowd's cheers erupted. Giving glory to the God whom she follows.

For Teresa, it's not about the crown. She'll be the first to remind you that it will eventually tarnish and grow dull.

Her moment on the stage will be forgotten. The dresses packed away. And she will still be God's daughter, influencing, loving, and serving . . . wherever He places her.

Teresa knows that God has a reason for every person she meets. She doesn't define herself by what people expect but by what God created her to be.[3]

But it wasn't easy. Throughout her year as Miss America, Teresa faced pressure and criticism from both sides. Some people thought she was too conservative. Some thought she was too liberal. Some critics said she was too pretty; others said she was too ugly.[4]

Nonstop speaking engagements and constant attacks from the media pushed Teresa into a deep depression. Suicide seemed an easy way out. She was falling apart emotionally and even considered jumping off a mountain.[5]

But Teresa didn't lose hope. Instead of taking her life, she reached out . . . and got help. With the help of counseling, medication, and a supportive community, Teresa now encourages other girls who live with depression.

Depression is not something to be embarrassed about, Teresa says. She urges anyone suffering from depression or considering suicide to seek help and to know that there is hope.[6]

Now twenty-one, Teresa is pursuing her college degree in government. She plans to go on to law school, become a Nebraska congresswoman, and run for president in 2028.

This woman is a rebel. She is rebelling against status and prestige . . . and harnessing the power of influence. Becoming a woman of integrity. A woman others can trust. A woman who is honest—and reaches out for help when she needs it.

A woman not defined by culture but who shapes it.

Teresa is chasing after the beauty of a life fully surrendered to God. The beauty of serving other people.

She dares to dream big.

Neither Feminism nor Slavery

"I am woman, hear me roar . . . " The 1970s pop song became an anthem for women's lib and feminism.[7] Women rallied together to let the world know they were created for more than to be barefoot, pregnant, in the kitchen, and "servicing" their husband.

"Freedom trash cans" at many rallies became places to get rid of aprons. Stockings. High heels. Tweezers. Curlers. Magazines like *Ladies' Home Journal* and *Playboy*. Women burned their bras and reveled in their newfound freedom.

I've got to admit, these women had some valid points. They rebelled against the idea that women are inferior. Weak. Unintelligent. They spoke up about abuse and domestic violence, and they championed women's education and public voice. It's hard to imagine that less than fifty years ago, women didn't have the right to go to certain universities. To be paid a fair wage. To pursue God's calling for them.

But much of the feminist voice has also been characterized by anger and disrespect toward men. As if all the problems in life come from the male gender. Just think about it. *Men*struate. *Men*opause. *Men*tal illness. *Men*ial. There's got to be some pattern here, right? Maybe the world would just be better off without men, some say.

I think we have taken it a bit too far, ladies. Culture has certainly oppressed women. Some men have abused their power to control. And sadly, a lot of the brokenness and struggle comes from bad theology and toxic faith.

Even today, the realities of sexual abuse, domestic violence, and rape are startling. Add to that the growing prevalence of pornography. Human trafficking. Sexual harassment. All these evils enslave and harm women—and I'm not trying to downplay that. As a Christian, I want to be on the front lines of advocating for women.

But that does not mean that all men are rapists . . . or that being a true woman requires hating the male gender. Hardening our hearts to love. Devaluing the wisdom of godly men. Rejecting the beauty of motherhood. Denying the tenderness, creativity, and nurture God has placed in our hearts.

It's easy to get caught in the cross fire between feminism, Hollywood, and religious dogma. To get confused and lose our way.

Who am I? And what's my life about? These are questions I wrestle with often.

It's easy to get caught in the cross fire between feminism, Hollywood, and religious dogma.

I'm not aiming to be like Gloria Steinem, who jokes, "A woman without a man is like a fish without a bicycle."[8] Belittling my fiancé Ben and denying the important role he plays in my life is not what it means to me to be a woman. Quite the opposite; I want to learn to love, honor, and respect him.

Kim Kardashian isn't my hero either. She told her fans that her seventy-two-day marriage just wasn't the fairy tale she had hoped for.[9] As I get ready to walk down the aisle, I'm not so much looking for a fairy tale (which doesn't exist!) as I am excited to spend the rest of my life—the fun, exciting times as well as the tough and challenging times—with my best friend.

And I'm not buying the misguided advice of those who misinterpret what it means to be a "help meet" in Genesis 2:18 (KJV). To make my husband happy and successful. To serve him and meet his every need—*no matter what*. That anything else—whether ministry, profession, or friendship—I find fulfillment in is sin.

This sort of religious dogma is oppressive, teaching women they should even endure mistreatment without protest and that abuse is their fault.

Excuse me? It's infuriating to see Scripture so misused and twisted. What a far cry this is from God's heart! Take one look at the life of Jesus: He cared for and loved women. He spoke up for them. He valued and honored them when others didn't.

I know I have a lot to learn about marriage, but not once does God's Word encourage men to demean, control, or abuse women. Not once.

Somewhere in the chaos, we can easily lose sight of who God created us to be.

In the Beginning

God made a woman. These words, taken from Genesis 2:22 (NIV), are the heart of our identity. If God wanted to, He could have made another man, but no—He chose to make woman. And my goodness, was she very different from man!

Just ask Adam. One look at her feminine beauty, and he said, "Whoa . . . man!"

Okay, maybe I took a little poetic license there, but seriously! God made us unique for a specific reason. Physical beauty. Emotional tenderness. Nurturing hearts. A deep longing to connect. These aren't random traits. Nor are they signs of weakness.

Far from it.

Each of our feminine strengths is an exquisite expression of who God is.

> Each of our feminine strengths is an exquisite expression of who God is.

"When it comes to the question of gender," psychologist Larry Crabb shares, "our culture is really screwed up. . . . In the middle of all this confusion, there's one question that stands out. *What does it mean to be a woman*?"[10]

Crabb continues, "A woman is most feminine to the degree that she relates in a way that reveals something wonderful about God that no man can as fully reveal."[11]

We as women uniquely reveal God's mercy, tenderness, and compassion to the world in a way that many men cannot. Wow! Now there's a responsibility to take seriously!

God made woman. It wasn't chance, but thoughtful purpose. When we can truly grab hold of this, it changes everything. We're freed from the lies of culture to be exactly who we were created to be . . . by God's design.

> It's not about equality. It's about men and women complementing each other, each revealing unique parts of who God is.

We are not equal with men—and we're not quite like men. We are women. It's not about equality. It's about men and women complementing each other, each revealing unique parts of who God is. And I want to celebrate that.

Too often, we let Hollywood and Madison Avenue shape our identities. Culture is continually trying to re-create us—either as man haters or weak-willed wimps.

Maybe you've been there. Independent and angry . . . *I don't need a man!* Or a ticking time bomb of insecurity . . . *I can't live without him!*

Either extreme is a cheap shot compared to our true destiny as God's daughters. Who wants to live a small, self-consumed life when we were created for so much more?

Graceful strength. Service rooted in love. Confidence from God alone.

A woman who is not defined by culture but who shapes it instead.

This is our calling—to be women of true beauty and influence. In our homes. In our families. With our friends. In our churches and communities.

"God made me a girl," Leslie Ludy writes. "And He did that on purpose. But He asks me to become the kind of girl who is actually useful to His kingdom purposes."[12]

And what does that look like? She continues:

> I need to become the sort of girl who is unafraid to poke my head into the battle of the ages and cry out, "Who is this uncircumcised Philistine who is blaspheming the armies of the living God?"
>
> God wants me to wrestle. God wants to stick grit in my girliness. He wants me to be prepared to tangle, to interlock my soul in this eternal combat—not with other girls, not with sweaty boys, but with Him, and with the otherworldly powers of darkness. He wants me to wrestle in prayer, to grab ahold of His great and precious promises and fight to see them unfurled in living reality on this Earth.[13]

Do you see what we've missed? It's not about dissing the male gender or denying our dreams. It's about living as God's daughters—bold, fearless, and free.

One Radical Woman

An entire year at the spa. Just imagine it: Moisturizing baths. Aromatic lotions. Hair treatments. Facials. Manicures and pedicures. Choice perfumes.

Not to mention being fitted for designer clothes and custom jewelry.

From the outside, it looked like a dating contest—the Old Testament version of *The Bachelor*. Only, these beautiful young women didn't voluntarily enter in the contest. They were taken from their homes. Ripped from the arms of family and friends.

Held in custody. Captives. All for one purpose—the king's pleasure. Xerxes was on the hunt for a new queen.

Who would it be? The world waited.

She was stunning and mysterious, this girl named Esther. Her dark eyes and beautiful figure caught the attention of Hegai, the man in charge. But more than anything, he was intrigued by her calm, kind, and caring heart.

There's something different about Esther. She stands out from all the other girls.

Luxurious rooms. Special food. Seven personal maids. Hegai made sure Esther had the best of everything.

But it didn't satisfy. Fear, anxiety, and aching loneliness became her daily companions.

Staring up at the night sky through an open window, Esther cried out to the God of her fathers: *Yahweh, I learned Your promises as a little girl. That You are with me. That You are my refuge and protector. Give me strength to be a light for You here. Give me wisdom, God . . . there seems no way out of this. And to sleep with the king . . . under Jewish law, I should be stoned. Please give me favor, and make my path straight.*

"Esther? It's time!" Hegai's words echoed down the hallway.

The royal palace. It was more ornate than she'd even dreamed. She tried to calm her racing heart as she opened the door to enter the king's inner chamber.

In a foreign land. An orphan. Forced into servitude. Separated from her cousin Mordecai, who was like a father to her. But God went before her, never forsaking His daughter.

"Esther was winning favor in the eyes of all who saw her. . . . The king loved Esther more than all the women, and she won grace and favor in his sight more than all the virgins, so that he set the royal crown on her head and made her queen."

Could a Jew really be queen of Persia?

But the story doesn't end there.

Her hands shook as she read the verdict: "to destroy, to kill, and to annihilate all Jews, young and old, women and children, in one day . . . and to plunder their goods."

The mark of the king's signet ring left no doubt. *It was the law.*

Esther's heart froze in fear. Horror and dismay clouded her mind.

What does this mean? Dear cousin Mordecai. My childhood friends. All to be murdered? And what about me? No one knows that I, too, am a Jew . . .

Esther was faced with a terrifying choice: to keep silent and watch the slaughter of those she loved or to speak up and likely be killed herself.

It's the ultimate question: self-preservation or self-sacrifice? To look out for ourselves or to take bold risks? To run and hide or to be rebellious and live free?

If I go to the king without being called, I could be put to death.

"Who knows whether you have not come to the kingdom for such a time as this?" Mordecai's words rang in Esther's ears as she looked out the palace window. The streets were teeming with Jewish people. Going to market. Coming home. Drawing water. Calling little ones home to rest from the hot sun.

The thought of these innocent people . . . dead . . . it made her nauseous. All the facial treatments, the stunning dresses . . . they all meant nothing now.

Could the fate of an entire people really rest in my hands? Me? An exile and an orphan?

Gathering all the courage she could muster, Esther spoke. "Go, gather all the Jews . . . hold a fast on my behalf, and do not eat or drink for three days."

She fought back the lump in her throat to continue. "Then I will go to the king, though it is against the law, and if I perish, I perish."

To defy the king. To risk her life. To beg for mercy.

In one moment, Esther made the giant leap from a beautiful girl to a woman of influence. From spa treatments and pampering to a bold stand against injustice and evil. From fighting for the crown to willingly laying her life down.

From fun and flirty to a faith that gave her confidence. Audacity. Bravery to walk straight into danger, knowing that she was not alone.

Esther wasn't a man hater or a victim. She didn't enter the king's courts shouting, "I am woman!" or burn any bras to prove her point.

Far from it! She called her friends together and got on her face before God—for three days straight. They wrestled in prayer. Grabbed hold of God's promises. Fought through emotional confusion to believe and follow God's leading.

It wasn't a glamorous or showy preparation; it was painful. Difficult. I'm sure in the midst of those prayers, the tears flowed. *God, please hear me! Go before me. Give me favor with the king!*

Soften his heart. Let him see the truth and have mercy on the Jewish people.

Rather than caving in the shadow of Xerxes' power, Esther rooted herself in the promises of a far greater King. *This* is the secret of a woman of God. She knows the source of her power—far greater than anything she can muster on her own.

Will this be my very last sunrise? As Esther put on her royal robes, she battled back feelings of despair. How different this walk was to Xerxes' court. Far from seducing the king, she was perhaps walking straight into her grave.

Fear gripped her heart as she entered the throne room. Deafening silence as she waited to catch the king's eye.

And then, she could hardly believe it . . . Xerxes smiled. Held out his golden scepter to welcome her.

"What is it, Queen Esther? What is your request? It shall be given you, even to the half of my kingdom."

Wisdom. Patience. Trust in God's timing. I wonder if Esther wanted to blurt it out right then and there: *Haman's trying to kill me . . . kill us all!*

But she didn't. Another mark of a true woman—self-control. She didn't need to manipulate, raise her voice, or use angry threats to make her point. Instead, she harnessed her incredible influence to invite and nurture.

Esther invited the king to a special dinner she prepared for him—and asked him to bring Haman as his honored guest.

The king was intrigued and honored. Who wouldn't want to spend the evening with such a beautiful woman?

One dinner . . . and then, after dinner, an invitation to still another special evening. Esther led by serving. By welcoming.

She wasn't hasty, thoughtless, or rude. Instead, Esther's presence exuded graceful strength. Discernment. Sensitivity to God's leading.

A second dinner party, and the moment came.

"If I have found favor in your sight, O king, and if it please the king, let my life be granted me for my wish, and my people for my request."

No dissing the king here. No attacking. Just a calm and honest request.

"For we have been sold," Esther explained to the king, "I and my people, to be destroyed, to be killed, and to be annihilated."

King Xerxes exploded, "Who is he, and where is he, who has dared to do this?"

Again, Esther stepped out in bold faith. No holding back or quivering in fear. She called it like it was.

"A foe and enemy! This wicked Haman!" Esther pointed to the king's good friend. Raging mad, Xerxes ordered for Haman to be hanged.

And Esther? She and Mordecai were given power to write a new law on the king's behalf. A law to protect their people—the Jews—and ensure their safety.

I love Esther's story because she is so human. Imperfect. Relatable. Just an ordinary girl who was taken captive and had some tough decisions to make. But all along, God was at work. He came through for Esther, and He will come through for us too.[14]

Esther saw through the fading promises of physical beauty and embraced a life of boldness and influence. Because no amount of spa treatments or sexual escapades can truly satisfy a woman's heart. Esther found her true identity as a woman of God.

To take a stand. To speak up. To become more than a pretty face, a seductive body, or a dinner host. To actually believe God's promises . . . and storm the gates of hell, if necessary. To risk everything to obey and trust God with the outcome. This is true womanhood.

Decisions, Decisions

In today's world, women like Esther are desperately needed. In families. In the church. In the community. In the corporate world.

God created each of us with unique talents and gifts, and while these may include being a wife and mother, that is not *all* that they include. God wants to use each of us where we are to make a difference in His kingdom—married or single. Our duty is not ultimately to our home or career; it's to serving God.

While our culture places a primary focus on a woman's career, the reality is that most—if not all—of us find ourselves in multiple life roles. I really like the word *vocation* to help describe this complexity, because it encompasses not only our current occupation but also every area of our life and life's work. Coming from the Latin root *vox*, or "voice," *vocation* has been described as "one's entire life lived in response to God's voice."[15]

This strikes at the core of our identity as God's daughters, even in the midst of changing seasons. For some of us, it's raising children. For others, it's teaching. Working in the medical field. As a lawyer. A corporate leader. In a governmental office. As an interior designer. A counselor. A marketing/PR specialist. A writer. An architect. Or a barista.

Rebekah Lyons writes, "If women aren't empowered to cultivate their uniqueness, we all suffer the loss of beauty, creativity and resourcefulness they were meant to contribute to the world."[16] In each season of life, we have the opportunity to cultivate our identity as a woman of God in diverse ways . . . by the way we love and serve.

What makes you feel alive? What has God placed in your heart? Whatever that is, pursue it. Harness it as a way to serve. And be faithful wherever God has placed you. I love what missionary Jim Elliot wrote: "Wherever you are, be all there! Live to the hilt every situation you believe to be the will of God."[17]

The world tries to tell us we can have it all, but the reality is, we can't. There is no such thing as a "superwoman" or "supermom." We all have limits. That's why it's important to prayerfully weigh our priorities, make intentional decisions, and hold things loosely.

While career is one significant way women can shape culture, it is certainly not the sum total of our vocation. Lilian Barger wisely points out, "Today with much more freedom to choose our own way in the world, we are more likely to lose ourselves in the process."[18] We have to be careful that we don't forget what matters most. Relationships. Time with family and friends. Serving our community. Impacting other people, not accomplishment. You can't get back time with your husband, kids, or friends that you gave up for a promotion.

As a young professional in the medical field, I've wrestled often between the career tracks of medical doctor (MD) and physician assistant (PA). I've spent many a night staring at the ceiling, thinking. Praying. Asking God for wisdom. Weighing the pros and cons.

We all have to prioritize at some point. On one hand, I want to take the longer track to MD. But after wrestling and seeking God about it, I see that, in my particular circumstances, becoming a PA will ultimately best equip me to pursue my vocation—to serve and help people who are in need while allowing me the flexibility in the future to invest in my children's lives and serve in medical missions.

One of the greatest gifts my parents gave me was making me a priority and spending time together. I want that for my kids.

On the heels of radical feminism, which dissed being a mom, I'm encouraged to see that the "baby bump" is back in style. In today's world, it doesn't have to be *either* career *or* family! But godly counsel is definitely needed along the way. I'm finding that I have to make some tough decisions, and I admit I can't do it all.

As you think about career options, I encourage you to consider not just your paycheck but what you ultimately want to invest your life in. Why not harness your career for God's kingdom? Since I went on my first mission trip to South America as a teenager, God gave me a huge passion for serving "the least of these" by providing medical care (Matthew 25:40 NIV). I say we start making decisions with the goals of serving, helping, and shaping culture, not just making a name for ourselves.

God's path for each of us is unique. That's why it's so critical to "tune in" to His calling rather than be swayed by the peer pressures of the world—or Christian culture, for that matter. If God is tugging at your heart to become an MD . . . or a lawyer . . . or a politician . . . or a fashion designer . . . or an engineer . . . or a business owner, I'd be the first to encourage you to go for it! We need Christian women who are culture shapers in every area of society!

I love Paul's encouragement in 1 Corinthians 7:17: "And don't be wishing you were someplace else or with someone else.

Where you are right now is God's place for you. Live and obey and love and believe right there."

As women, we need to be intentional about developing into who God created us to be. And we must remember that there is more to our calling as women of God than simply the job we currently hold. We all may fill multiple roles—wife, mother, employee, friend, just to name a few—so our vocation will look different for each of us. But we need to get serious about seeking God rather than blindly buying into what culture says. Don't let anyone tell you that you have to fit a specific mold to be successful.

> Don't let anyone tell you that you have to fit a specific mold to be successful.

Wisdom is needed. That's why we need older, godly women speaking into our lives. Not ads. Not chick flicks. Not *Seventeen* or *Vogue*. We need mentors who will challenge us. Women who will speak truth into our lives and disciple us along the way.

What's Holding You Back?

Teresa, Esther, and you. As a woman, you have unique power to influence others. To lead by serving. To break down the lies of culture and share the love of Christ.

What dreams has God put in your heart? Are you holding back in insecurity, fear, or doubt? Teresa Scanlan reveals that too many women use age as an excuse, claiming they're too young or too old to follow their God-sized dreams. Instead, she urges women of all ages to step up to the plate![19]

To become who God created us to be as women, we need to rebel against both extremes.

Rebel against the radical feminist movement that hates and degrades men. Rebel against the belief that faithfulness and commitment to one man for life is old-fashioned. Rebel against the idea that being a mom isn't important.

At the same time, we've got to rebel against the religious dogma often perpetuated in the name of "submission" that robs women of their identity and purpose. We've got to see this toxic faith for the sham that it is . . . and speak some truth that sets women free!

God made you and me as *women*. That means something— more than just biological differences. So don't let life just happen. Don't let culture tell you what to do. Seek God and take time to consider the passions and talents He's put in your heart. Like Esther, He has created you for such a time as this.

But remember, *it's not ultimately about you*. It's really about God working in and through you to love and serve other people. There's no need to make a name for yourself—you are already His daughter. So invest

> There's no need to make a name for yourself— you are already His daughter. So invest yourself in building His kingdom, not yours.

yourself in building His kingdom, not yours—whether working in a corporate setting, leading a Bible study, changing diapers, working as a missionary, competing in a Miss America pageant, or cooking dinner for your family.

Neither feminism nor slavery. Let's choose to rebel against a culture that tries to define success for us—and choose to let God define success for us instead.

CHAPTER SIX

Sex and Sexy

Sex can be a handy substitute for authentic
intimacy. . . . But when the relationship
comes unglued, so do the feelings.

—*Jim Hancock and Kara Powell*

S TOP RUNNING TRACK RACES and go find some sex!"[1]

That's the kind of advice fans gave to Olympic hurdler Lolo Jones, who, at thirty years old, was still a virgin.

When Lolo came in fourth place at the 2012 London Olympics—just 0.10 seconds behind the bronze medalist—Twitter exploded with abrasive comments. Fans claimed that her virginity caused her to lose the race, and followed insulting tweets with hashtags such as #lolojoneshater and #Sexisforwinners.[2]

Wow! Talk about vicious! But as a female athlete, Lolo is no stranger to such criticism.

Lolo admits she's been tempted. A number of people have told her that having sex would make her run faster. But she's still choosing to wait until marriage.[3]

C'mon. What makes Lolo so strong in her commitment?

She's seen just how heart-wrenching the alternative can be. Her parents were together for twenty years—and then they split up.[4]

Lolo grew up in a single-parent home with five siblings. Her father was in and out of jail, so her mom worked two jobs to try to keep food on the table. When they didn't have money for rent, her family would move, Lolo remembers.[5]

As a little girl, Lolo's life was unstable. Unpredictable. And constantly changing. Growing up in poverty, Lolo went to five different elementary schools and three middle schools. Once, when her family was homeless, they even took shelter in a church basement.

Lolo's dad was out of the picture, and her mom worked long hours. Not exactly the model Christian family, huh?

Lolo knows what family difficulty looks like. It's all she knew as a kid.

But Lolo has chosen a very different life for herself when it comes to sex and relationships. "I don't have a hard time finding dates, but [it's] hard finding the right one to date," she said.[6] Sex is a gift Lolo wants to give to her husband. She says staying a virgin is the hardest thing she's ever done—even harder than training for the Olympics. She admits she is judged a lot. A lot of guys don't return her calls after they find out.[7]

Lolo's right. In today's culture, sexual purity is often laughed at. From TV shows to college parties, virgins are viewed as weirdos. Freaks. Narrow-minded bigots who are missing out on all the "fun."

And Lolo isn't the only one to come under fire. American quarterback and conservative Christian Tim Tebow recently caught the eye of AshleyMadison.com, the world's leading website for finding an affair. Sports and sex go hand in hand, they touted.[8]

Incredulously, the online dating service put out a one-million-dollar bounty for anyone who managed to sleep with Tebow.[9]

In a culture where hooking up is normal, Lolo is a rebel . . . and Tebow too. Rebelling against the pressure to have sex, even when they're being offered it left and right. Defying the lie we so often buy into—that "no date will stick around if I don't give them some."

This kind of commitment flies in the face of our culture's cheap view of sex. Both Lolo and Tebow have been dissed by teammates. Mocked by the media. Attacked and belittled on social media and the news.

Yet both of these athletes have stood their ground. No apologies. No compromises. Far from dissing sex or pretending she doesn't want it, Lolo views it as immensely powerful. Valuable. Beautiful. Intimate.

Something worth saving.

Flaunting Our "Stuff"

Lace. Frills. And a little tease. As I looked at the pile of gift bags and Victoria's Secret boxes at my lingerie wedding shower, I smiled.

Candles. Romance. Mystery. Delight. His eyes—only for me.

Okay, let me just say it . . . I can't wait.

Seriously.

As I write this, I'm just a few months out from getting married, and believe me, I've been thinking about it. A lot.

> There doesn't seem to be any mystery about sex these days. It's everywhere.

Truth is, there doesn't seem to be any mystery about sex these days. It's everywhere. Miley Cyrus twerking in a nude bikini. Katy Perry showing off topless for *Esquire* magazine. Rihanna posing like a stripper, complete with dollar bills stuffed in her underwear. Kim Kardashian, who first caught the public eye when her sex tape surfaced online.

We know how to flaunt our stuff. Butt. Boobs. Some call it "sexual freedom," "liberation," and "progress." Really?

Casual sex is "in." Sexual prowess has become a rite of passage—a mark of becoming a woman. One cultural researcher points out that hookups are becoming common in popular culture. People engage in sexual behaviors, ranging from kissing to oral sex and intercourse, without any promise of or desire for a lasting relationship. Hookups provide the experience of sex with no strings attached.[10]

Or so they say. But does it work?

One thirteen-year-old reported feeling dirty after agreeing to have sex with a classmate. She was surprised to discover afterward that she wasn't important to him at all.[11]

Ever been there?

Fifty-six percent of teenage girls think that one of the most important things they can do is attract boys and look sexy.[12]

Sexting is quickly becoming the norm in middle and high school. It's the era of "rainbow parties," where girls come armed with an array of lip gloss, and guys try to gather a rainbow of colors through oral sex.[13]

Nearly one in three young adults will hook up with someone they just met today, and over half will hook up with someone they consider a close friend.[14]

One-third of all visits to online porn sites are made by—you guessed it—ladies. In fact, 13 percent of women admit to accessing porn while at work.[15]

This obsession with sex is out of control. And not just among adults. Sex is even robbing us of our childhood. When five-year-old girls—barely more than toddlers—are giving oral sex to other kids at preschool, something is gravely wrong.[16]

When high schoolers stand by and let a girl be raped at a party, as in the Steubenville, Ohio, rape case,[17] we have to stop and reconsider where we are headed.

This is the craziness our culture is selling us. And it is killing us.

Adele's heartbreaking songs remind us that love hurts. The intimate moment of sex never lasts. Things fall apart. Guys walk away.

And we are left with deep emotional wounds. Questions. Broken hearts. Nearly 80 percent of women in one study regretted their decision after hooking up.[18]

College students reported feeling embarrassed. Emotional. Disrespected. Anger. Self-hatred. Loneliness. [19]

Maybe you feel the same way. Maybe you've been chasing sexual pleasure and gotten lost in it, always searching for another guy. Another night in bed. Another orgasm. Maybe you've even gone so far as to explore sexual encounters with other girls.

Or perhaps your story is quite different. Maybe you were abused—sex was forced on you as a young girl. Maybe you carry the memories of rape. The weight of an abortion. The daily reminder of a sexually transmitted infection, which inflicts 50 percent of sexually active young adults.[20]

Or maybe you grew up in a legalistic religious home. Maybe you were told lies about sex—that it was evil, gross, and dirty. Maybe you find sex repulsive, and you're considering putting down this book right now.

When it comes to sex, many of us have been hurt or left confused in one way or another. Enter *Sex and the City*. "If you believe in love," Skipper suggests in the book, "you're setting yourself up to be disappointed."[21]

> When it comes to sex, many of us have been hurt or left confused in one way or another.

"All those men who end up disappointing you. After a while, you don't even want to have feelings anymore," the book's narrator moans. "You just want to get on with your life."[22]

"I have no sex and no romance," Skipper admits. "Who needs it? Who needs all these potential problems like disease and pregnancy? I have no problems. No fear of disease, psychopaths, or stalkers. Why not just be with your friends and have real conversations and a good time?"[23]

They make a point—maybe sex isn't worth the heartache.

You Might Be Surprised

But what if everything we've been told about sex is a lie?

What if all those steamy sex scenes in the movies are staged? What if sex isn't the glue that will keep your boyfriend around but, rather, the very thing that could destroy your relationship?

What if your sexuality as a woman is about more than just the erotic? And what if all that narrow-minded talk in some churches about sex being "hush-hush" is wrong too?

Growing up in a conservative family, I heard a lot about purity—Sunday school, youth group, True Love Waits conferences, countless lectures and sermons—you've probably heard the spiel.

"Don't have sex with your boyfriend, or . . ."

Or what?

The problem is, these talks left many of us hanging. Most of what we've heard about sex is "don't." Rules. Threats. Fear-driven messages intended to keep your clothes on and a penny between your knees.

At times, it seems like the world has all the fun.

> What if there really is something more to sex?

But what if there really is something more to sex? If there's one thing I've learned over the past few years, it's the importance of healthy questioning. Even in the church. We can so easily get sucked into worldly or legalistic lies and miss out on the life God intended for us to live as His daughters.

Read the following statement and answer—true or false: "The highest levels of sexual satisfaction were reported by individuals who were in married, monogamous relationships."[24]

You might be surprised, but the answer is true.

Research shows that the best sex is married sex—in the safety and freedom of a committed, loving intimate relationship.

You know what else surprised me? Married couples who connect spiritually rate each other as better lovers, and those who pray together report having more "ecstasy" in their sex lives.[25]

Naked and unashamed. No holding back. No guilt. No fear. No waking up with regrets the next morning.

What if sexual intimacy—with one man, for life—was one of the greatest gifts God ever created for you and me to enjoy?

I know; it sounds pretty radical. Perhaps even unrealistic.

You might be saying, "Megan, I'm sorry, but I don't live in Eden. There is no 'putting my sexuality to sleep' until God brings the right guy."

I agree with you. I have sexual desires—and if you're honest with yourself, you do too. Whether or not you've acted on them, God created you as an innately sexual being.

And that is beautiful.

Since you and I are sexual beings, what do we do with *that*?

I believe that sex is a God-given appetite. As women, we were uniquely created to be sexy, beautiful, and alluring. And there is great power in that. We long to captivate. To be romanced, pursued, and swept off our feet.

God put these things in our hearts—they are good and godly desires. Gary Thomas points out, "God made flesh, and when God made flesh, he created some amazing sensations."[26]

> Sadly, in many Christian circles, our sexuality as women has been ignored or silenced.

Sadly, in many Christian circles, our sexuality as women has been ignored or silenced. Many of us were introduced to sex in awkward or negative situations. Sex has been labeled as "evil" and "dangerous." And this is simply not true. We've perverted what God intended for pleasure.

I know a lot of young women who carry deep emotional wounds because of sexual betrayal. They may have used sex to try to keep a guy around, but it didn't work for long. When he lost interest or cheated on them, they were heartbroken.

They, like the women in *Sex and the City*, have stopped trusting men and doubt that sex could ever be safe or emotionally meaningful again. They may turn to other things to satisfy their sexual desires but have given up on sex with one man—for life.

I also know other women who live in constant shame and guilt. They feel awkward and dirty about sexual intimacy with their husbands. Whether because of past sexual abuse or growing up in a legalistic church environment, they view themselves as asexual, ugly, and think of sex as sinful and wrong. Sure, they may endure it, but are they experiencing sex as God intended?

We must rebel against both extremes. We've got to rebel against the idea that we're only sex objects and actually start respecting ourselves! Setting some boundaries. Breaking up with guys who pressure or manipulate us to cave in.

> We've got to rebel against the idea that we're only sex objects and actually start respecting ourselves!

At the same time we've got to also rebel against the idea that good Christian girls don't care about or enjoy sex. I want to be attractive. I want to be noticed. To turn my husband on. And to enjoy what God says is beautiful between a husband and wife.

One Radical Woman

Romance. Desire. Pursuit. Intimacy. It's the love story we all dream about. And yes, it's in the Bible. Not a trashy romance novel or a graphic chick flick.

The Shulamite woman—King Solomon's bride—expresses her sexuality in a beautiful, God-honoring way. She's sensuous. Sexy. Alluring. And yes, godly.

His strong arms around me. His soft kisses on my forehead. It's all so surreal. Like a dream. He chose me—just an ordinary country girl. And he—the king!

No holding back here. "Kiss me—full on the mouth!" she whispers to her husband. "Yes! For your love is better than wine, headier than your aromatic oils. . . . Take me away with you!"

This man has captured my heart. Swept me off my feet. He turns me on with his gentle, tender love. I know that I am safe. Treasured. Loved. I know that I am his.

"My lover stands above the young men in town. All I want is to sit in his shade, to taste and savor his delicious love. He took me home with him for a festive meal, but his eyes feasted on *me!*"

His eyes are only for me, and I delight to give him myself— holding nothing back. To unveil the mystery of my beauty. To flaunt it. To drive him crazy with desire.

And boy, does he enjoy the moment!

"Your beauty is too much for me—I'm in over my head," Solomon gasps. "I'm not used to this! I can't take it in."

He tells her, "You're so beautiful, my darling, so beautiful, and your dove eyes are veiled by your hair as it flows and shimmers. . . . Your lips are jewel red, your mouth elegant and inviting . . . Your breasts are like fawns, twins of a gazelle, grazing among the first spring flowers. The sweet, fragrant curves of your body, the soft, spiced contours of your flesh invite me, and I come. I stay until dawn."

Whew! Getting a little on the steamy side. (And she's certainly not wearing a sack.) Bow chicka wow wow!

My beauty invites. Seduces. Captivates. This is what I was created for. I give myself freely to my one and only love—no pressure, no guilt, no holding back. Naked and unashamed.

"You're beautiful from head to toe, my dear love, beautiful beyond compare, absolutely flawless. . . . You're a secret garden, a private and pure fountain. Body and soul, you are paradise, a whole orchard of succulent fruits . . . a garden fountain, sparkling and splashing."

Pure. Chaste. Saved only for him. My body is his. And he delights in me.

Solomon boasts that he has the most amazing wife. "There's no one like her on earth, never has been, never will be. She's a woman beyond compare. My dove is perfection, pure and innocent as the day she was born."

My purity is my gift to him. What his eyes see, no other man will. My lips are saved only for him. His hands caress my undefiled beauty.

"I'm about to faint with love!" this bride cries out. "His left hand cradles my head, and his right arm encircles my waist! . . . My lover is mine, and I am his."

His tender touch leaves me ecstatic. My beloved knows me intimately and goes out of his way to thrill me. But it's not just that. He's wise, kind, and respectable. He's a man of character I know I can trust—with everything.

"Everything about him delights me, thrills me through and through!"

I love him—not just for his charm and good looks, but because of who he is as a man. He protects me, takes care of me, and lets me lean into his strength when I have none. I am safe. I am loved. I am his—and our intimacy is an expression of that bond!

"I am my lover's. I'm all he wants. I'm all the world to him! Come, dear lover. . . . Love-apples drench us with fragrance, fertility surrounds, suffuses us, fruits fresh and preserved that I've kept and saved just for you, my love."

No doubt about it—this gal is talking about S-E-X! She's describing the passionate love and sweet intimacy she experiences with the man she has committed her life to.[27]

Hot and holy. Alluring. Powerful. Sensual. Pleasurable. Fulfilling. Sacred.

This is sexual intimacy as God intended it. Not an offhanded expression of physical attraction with just any guy, but a powerful, intimate experience of oneness and delight with her husband. Not just biological parts fitting together, but a true soul connection.

Sex is not just physical—it's emotional and spiritual too. Gary Thomas writes, "Our God, who is spirit (John 4:24), can be found behind the very physical panting, sweating, and pleasurable entangling of limbs and body parts. He doesn't turn away."[28]

In fact, an ancient Jewish text describes sexual intimacy as "a mystical experience of meeting with God . . . 'becom[ing] partners with God in the act of creation.'" He continues, "When a man unites with his wife in holiness, the Shekinah is between them."[29]

What's *Shekinah*? It is the presence of God—the same word used when Moses met with God face-to-face (Exodus 24:15–18).

It is precisely because sex is so powerful that the woman in this story warns us: "Don't excite love, don't stir it up, until the time is ripe—and you're ready" (Song of Solomon 2:7).

There is a time for love to be awakened. And then to get lost in it—with our husband. To be completely satisfied in his love for us.

This radical woman speaks directly into our lives, in a world where sex is cheap. We've reduced sex to cleavage, booty, and "losing it" in the backseat of the car.

God isn't the one who perverts sex. We do. We often settle for a cheap imitation of authentic intimacy.

From Shame to Sexual Wholeness

"But I've blown it, Megan," you may say. "The thrill is gone. The beauty of what I want is gone. I feel dirty, guilty, and used up."

None of us is immune to desire. I've had countless discussions with godly Christian women—friends of mine—who broke their purity vows. Cheated on their boyfriends or husbands. Got caught up in porn.

In a moment of passion, they made an empty decision.

And the morning after, shame settles in like a dark cloud. Condemnation. Regret. Self-hatred. Crippling lies.

You're a slut. You're worthless. God could never forgive you.

Maybe you can relate.

Why not do it again? You've already screwed up your life.

At least it will numb the pain. At least—for that moment—you won't be alone.

Pursuing purity is tough. But even more painful can be the lies we start believing about ourselves as a result of sexual failures. Lies that damage and enslave us.

It tears at our souls and our identity as women. Before long, we give up trying. Give up fighting.

We reduce ourselves to sex objects, thinking that sex is all there is to femininity. Our identities become wrapped up in turning a guy's head. We way overdo the makeup. Flaunt our stuff. Get a little kinky.

We play the game.

And sure, it can feel good in the moment. But lying in bed awake at night, we ache inside.

Ache for something more.

The Bible says, "In sexual sin we violate the sacredness of our own bodies, these bodies that were made for God-given and God-modeled love, for 'becoming one' with another" (1 Corinthians 6:18).

So, what if you're no longer a virgin? What if you struggle because you were sexually abused? How do you go forward from here? And will God restore you?

Absolutely.

If this is your story, I want you to know God offers you grace, forgiveness, and hope. You are not alone. God wants to redeem your sexuality.

> You are not alone. God wants to redeem your sexuality.

Jesus said that healing is a choice. His words are a soothing balm to our shame-sick souls.

Remember the woman who was caught in adultery? "Neither do I condemn you," He said. "Go now and leave your life of sin" (John 8:11 NIV).

Healing starts with honesty about where we are. About where we've failed. No more excuses or passing the buck. No more hiding, pretending, or lies.

The Bible is right—sexual sin violates the sacredness of our own bodies. But this is not the end of the story. We serve a God who longs to redeem and heal—to bring beauty out of brokenness. To turn our shame and failures into a powerful testimony!

After we've failed, Satan tries to sell us the lie that we're "damaged goods." And I say, no way! That is a flat-out lie.

"Leave your life of sin," Jesus says. Whether it's sleeping with your boyfriend, watching porn, or even just looking to guys for affirmation rather than being confident in who God created you to be, change is possible. And it starts with making a commitment to stop drinking the Kool-Aid.

Start fresh. Start today.

Surrender your sexual failures to God. He's waiting to restore you with grace, mercy, and forgiveness.

I know how much my dad loves me and how forgiving he is. Take the most loving father you know and he cannot even begin to measure up to God. God's grace, love, and forgiveness will always outweigh our mistakes.

Enough is enough! Kick shame to the curb. We were created for so much more.

To be hot and holy. Fully alive. Confident. Free.

So how can we enjoy and cultivate true intimacy in a world that's gone sex crazy? I don't think we can fully enjoy our sexuality or intimacy of any kind unless we protect it.

You are worth more than just your bra size.

You're not a juicy piece of meat to satisfy a man—you are a woman, beautifully and uniquely created by God. In fact, if any guy tries to use sex to pressure or control you, walk away. No, run away. You deserve better. You matter. You are beautiful and alluring. And somewhere out there is a guy who will value and treasure you for that. Who will work to win and woo

> You're not a juicy piece of meat to satisfy a man—you are a woman, beautifully and uniquely created by God

your heart—to build authentic intimacy and a deep emotional connection.

And if you are dating, let me encourage you to establish some good old-fashioned boundaries—both physically and emotionally. Don't lead yourself or your boyfriend into temptation! And also pray for each other to grow closer to Christ and resist the temptation to believe the culture's lies. One thing that really helped Ben and me when we were dating was to pray together, both at the beginning and the end of the date.

Ben and I also read Scripture together regularly, trying to keep our minds, hearts, and hormones focused on what it means to be truly in love with each other. At the end of the day, my focus is about falling more and more in love with Christ and realizing that God has given me the gift of this man—His precious son—to get to know. When I began to see our relationship at that level, it changed everything. After all, when I truly want the best for Ben, it's harder to pressure him to sin sexually.

Developing Your Sexy Side

"Sex and being sensual starts in your heart, Megan." My dad always has the best advice when it comes to relationships.

Despite the popularity of soft-porn books like *Fifty Shades of Grey*, sexuality is about more than just the erotic. More than just having sexual intercourse. Doug Rosenau and Michael Todd Wilson point out that our sexuality includes "our general sexual desire and gender makeup that propel each of us to seek out intimate connection—with another person, with a spouse or with God.

"Sexuality describes *who we are* more than what we do," they suggest. Stop and think about it: Your soft and strong traits. Your desires with urges and attractions. Your social interactivity, with flirtatiousness and playfulness. The set of values that direct your relational interactions.[30]

All of this—and more—are part of your sexuality.

What does it mean, then, to honor God with our sexuality, whether married or single?

I'm sure you've met a gorgeous, well-dressed woman before who was annoying and difficult. Her attitude was a turnoff, and she was anything but sexy.

Think about it. Anyone can walk around half-naked. We call that trashy.

Sexiness is more than just the size or shape of your body.

Yet, "The media reinforces the stereotype that the external appearance and a sexy body trump inner beauty and a woman's internal character."[31]

No wonder we're left confused and searching.

"Women experience an internal tug-of-war between the world and the Church. The world communicates impossible messages about femininity that combine a 'Barbie' sexiness with a 'successful woman who plays like the boys' in the cooperate arena. Meanwhile, the Church sometimes leans too heavily to the other extreme."[32]

It takes courage to rebel—against both extremes. I was encouraged recently to discover a new women's fashion and life-style magazine that is doing just that!

"Less of who you should be. More of who you are."[33] That's the motto for *Verily*, a magazine that—believe it or not—has banned the use of Photoshop on its models. No airbrushing or tummy tucking here.

Just genuine, natural beauty. Personality. Individuality.

In a refreshing rebrand of "sexy," cofounders Kara Eschbach and Janet Sahm believe the unique features of women—including freckles, wrinkles, and curves—are part of beauty and should be celebrated, not Photoshopped out.[34]

Wow. Way to go, Kara and Janet!

In a world obsessed with airbrushed images and sickly skinny models, it takes poise, tact, and intentionality to develop what Erica Tan and Anna Maya call "soul-sexy femininity."[35]

> True sexiness is confidence in the way God made you— soul, spirit, and body.

True sexiness is confidence in the way God made you— soul, spirit, and body.

Right now, you may not feel very beautiful or sexy. Maybe it's mistakes from your past speaking—choices you made that left you feeling dirty and trashy.

But I say, hold your head high. You are God's precious daughter!

It's important to take care of yourself. Work out. Find fashions that accentuate your body type. Get a cute haircut. Find a makeup style you like. Get in touch with your femininity, and please don't hide your beauty in a sack!

> Being sexy is not *just* about your appearance. Is your heart beautiful?

Being sexy is not *just* about your appearance. Is your heart beautiful? Are you caring? Warm? Nurturing? Responsive? Emotionally mature? Confident? Gracious? Secure in who you are as a woman?

As we begin to develop our sexy side, we need ask ourselves some hard questions:

- Who am I as a woman? How do I express that in my fashion and appearance?
- What am I looking for? What kind of guy do I want to attract?
- Do I really want to spend my life trying to fit into the culture's idea of "sexy"?
- What message do I want to communicate by how I dress and act?

And we need to stop making comparisons too. C'mon, we've all done it. *Does that dress look sexy on her or what? Ugh, I am so fat.*

When we compare ourselves with other women, we "diminish our unique identity and self-worth."[36] Each woman's sexiness is unique and created by God. There is no one-size-fits-all—in dresses or in beauty!

Settle down. Relax. Embrace who you are. There's nothing more beautiful and sensual than a woman who's confident in who she is.

Godliness . . . Back in Style!

Supermodels. Porn stars. Let's be honest—these women don't exist in real life anyway, and most of the time they are nothing more than computer-modified images.

Let's develop a soul-sexy femininity that makes us not only visually appealing but also inviting and intriguing. Alluring and mysterious.

Classy, not cheap.

Persuasive, but not provocative.

A woman after God's own heart.

Find creative ways to express your soul-sexy femininity, but "don't excite love, don't stir it up, until the time is ripe" (Song of Solomon 8:4). Not until you've got a wedding ring on your finger and that man all to yourself.

> Anyone can have sex. But it takes intentionality to build a real relationship that will last!

Anyone can have sex. But it takes intentionality to build a real relationship that will last!

I'm not saying this is easy. I'll be honest. Even with the man of my dreams, it's tough not to cross physical boundaries we've established. Sexual thoughts and desires are hard to control. But, like Lolo Jones said, I don't just want physical love; I want soul connection.

I want the Song of Solomon experience of sexual intimacy in marriage—don't you?

No matter what your past, you can begin making choices today to develop a lifestyle of purity.

Anything that gets in the way of that needs to go! Let's bring holiness back in style.

Soul sexiness will not only attract an honorable and godly man—rather than a jerk—and make you beautiful walking down the aisle on your wedding day but it is a sexiness that will endure. It will mature, blossom, and grow even more beautiful and intimate over time.

Who wouldn't want that kind of love and sex life?

CHAPTER SEVEN

From Facebook to Face-to-Face

Friendship is a deep oneness that
develops when two people, speaking
the truth in love to one another, journey
together to the same horizon.

—*Tim Keller*

BLINDING LIGHTS. Chalk on her hands. Her heart racing. The dull roar of the crowds. Millions watching from around the world.

After ten years and eighteen thousand hours of training, it had all come down to this moment—the 2012 Olympics.

But she was not alone.

Family. Friends. Teammates. Her coach. Her church.

In her lowest moments, they all encouraged her to keep fighting and never give up.[1]

Born with a rare blood disease, gymnast Gabby Douglas has an unlikely story—and she had plenty of opportunities to quit along the way.

The first "home" she ever knew was a blue Dodge van, parked in the corner of a rundown lot. A malnourished infant. A broken family. And a dad who didn't care.

But as a child Gabby was a fighter, not a victim. She was motivated. Determined. And she dared to dream. From one-handed cartwheels as a three-year-old, Gabby quickly progressed to winning regional and state gymnastic competitions.

Under the pressure of training and competing, Gabby quickly realized that willpower alone could only take her so far. She relied on a support system of friends and family who stood by her when she needed them the most, during the tough times.[2]

Gabby is anything but a self-made woman. Rebelling against our individualistic culture, she took the risk to be vulnerable. Honest. To build real, authentic relationships.

Inspired and intimidated. That's how Gabby had felt watching the 2008 Olympics—just four years earlier.

"I can never do that," she sighed, flopping down on the couch.

But Gabby's mom, Natalie, believed in her when the young athlete doubted herself.

Her mom taught her never to say "I can't." Instead, her mom would encourage Gabby to say, "That looks like a hard skill, but one I can learn."[3]

Gabby says her mom has influenced her so much. She taught Gabby to be a fighter and consistently supported her, making her journey to the Olympics possible.[4]

To compete on an Olympic level, Gabby needed to work with a world-renowned coach, which meant training in Iowa—thousands of miles away from her family.

Fourteen-year-old Gabby tried to be brave. But she was afraid. Alone. Homesick.

Is it really worth it? she wondered.

But rather than wallowing in loneliness, Gabby took the risk to reach out to her host parents for help and support. And she discovered an amazing blessing. Missy was like a second mom to Gabby, and her host family was like a second family.[5]

Her new coach, Liang Chow, was no different. Chow challenged her like never before, but he also truly cared. He pushed Gabby to excel, and she trusted him.[6]

Gabby sought out people she could trust, and she allowed them to speak into her life. To shape her. To challenge her. To hold her accountable.

Then it all unraveled.

Just months before she was set to compete in the 2012 Olympics, Gabby was done. Discouraged. Burnt out. Ready to quit.

She called her mom. "I feel so alone!" she sobbed.[7]

"Gymnastics is not my passion anymore. . . . I can get a job at Chick-fil-A. . . . I just want to be a normal teenage kid. I am so homesick. I just want to come home."[8]

And in that moment, Gabby's family and friends rallied around her. They believed in her. Encouraged her. Prayed for her.

Flash forward to August 2, 2012. A rainy Thursday afternoon in London.

In that moment before she took to London's Wembley Arena floor, Gabby's mind drifted back to all the double shifts her mom had worked to pay for gymnastics. The hundreds of hours she spent in training. The two years she spent apart from her family. The day, seven months earlier, when she almost gave it all up. . . . In an instant, everything was worth it.[9]

At just sixteen years old, Gabby not only walked away with two gold medals but became the first African American woman to win the all-around Olympic gold medal.

Along the way, Gabby was bullied for her ethnic heritage. Told to get cosmetic surgery because of her flat nose. Criticized for her funky hairstyles.

Yet she never caved to peer pressure. She told critics she wasn't going to change how she wore her hair, so they might as well just stop talking about it.[10]

Wow. That's a radical woman! A woman who knows who she is and doesn't get sucked into gossip. Rumors. Petty arguments.

As a young girl, long before she held a gold medal in her hands, Gabby made a critical decision. To let people in. To intentionally surround herself with a community of love and support.

Friends and mentors who would challenge her to be her best. She didn't waste time with people who would distract, pressure, or tear her down. Nor did she change who she was to fit in with the crowd.

Gabby is a woman of grit. Strength. Character. Faith. And humility.

Far from making a name for herself, Gabby points back to the true source of her success: God made it all possible, Gabby says. She gives Him all the glory for her success. And, of course, she points out that she couldn't have done it without the support of her family, coaches, and host family beside her the whole way.[11]

Gabby's tribute to her family is powerful:

To my mom: I couldn't have accomplished my dream without your constant support, sacrifice, and belief in me. I love you with all of my heart.

To my sister Arielle: Since the day you convinced Mom to put me in gymnastics, you've never stopped cheering for me.

To my sister Joyelle: You have prayed for me endlessly
and encouraged me even more than that. My life
just wouldn't be the same without you in it.

To my brother Johnathan: You have always been and
still are my best friend. Thank you for refusing to
let me stop fighting.[12]

Talk about a girl who values relationships!

"I just pray that God keep me humble and keep me grounded.
I don't want to be this on top diva. I want to be this role model,"
she said. "I want to be that blessing on other people."[13]

Gabby Douglas is not the "victim" of a broken home. Nor is
she a power-hungry star. She's an ordinary young woman who
dared to believe that God had created her for more.

More than a girl whose dad didn't care.

More than the future predicted by that blue Dodge van she
first called home.

Gabby dared to rebel against the bitterness and fear that
taunted, *Don't trust. Don't open up. Don't ask for help. They're
eventually going to leave—just like your dad did.*

I'm sure these thoughts went through Gabby's mind. Maybe
you've been there too.

Yet she fought for a different perspective. She fought to
trust. To love. To open up her heart. To get back up and try

again when she failed. To be a blessing and a role model to other girls.

"Hard days are the best because that's when champions are made," Gabby challenges us. "If you push through the hard days, then you can get through anything."[14]

That's core strength—strength I want in my life too! Strength to resist peer pressure. To rebel rather than follow the crowd.

Let's create a new culture that values gut honesty. Accountability. And real relationships.

> Let's create a new culture that values gut honesty. Accountability. And real relationships.

Hashtags and Followers

"Yes, the Internet is taking up time you used to spend with actual people." The title of the newspaper article caught my eye.[15] I was intrigued—I'm the worst about killing time on Facebook.

In today's world, connections are a dime a dozen. A recent study found that millennials often have at least five hundred Facebook "friends."

If you could call them that.

In reality, it's often quite a different story. Think about it. We barely know the majority of these people beyond their witty status updates and regular selfie photos. *Me and my morning coffee.*

Me and my new work outfit. Me and my boyfriend. Oh, and my dinner—in case you were wondering what I ate today.

Sure, it's fun to scroll through our news feeds and see what's going on in everyone else's lives. So we grab our phones before we roll out of bed. We scan social media sites at stoplights. While waiting in line. On coffee breaks. Even in the bathroom. It's addicting. And it definitely makes us feel "connected" in the moment.

Facebook. Twitter. Instagram. It's how we do relationships these days.

But when life falls apart—when you lose your job or you get that dreaded call from home or the test results come back positive—then what? When you, like Gabby, want to give up and throw in the towel, who will be there for you?

Please hear me on this: I am not bashing social media. In fact, I really enjoy seeing snapshots into my friends' lives. But there's a danger too. Comparison. Envy. Jealousy. Discontent. It's almost inevitable.

When you're working hard to pay off student loans and your college roommate posts a bazillion pictures of her epic backpacking trip in Europe that her parents paid for. Or when your high school friends post album after album of engagement photos . . . wedding photos . . . followed shortly by baby photos . . .

> When you, like Gabby, want to give up and throw in the towel, who will be there for you?

and you are still single and waiting. Not to mention the relationship status change when your ex finds his "true love."

Ugh. I hate that feeling. It's an icky somehow-I-missed-out-and-now-my-life-is-a-total-failure pity party. Ever been there?

It's a strange contradiction. In a world that's connected 24/7, we feel more alone than ever. We know lots of information about people, but do we have real relationships with people who will be there for us no matter what? Or are we just more lonely, anxious, and worried than ever? One commentator points out that we spend a lot of our time building large networks of shallow connections instead of investing in a few deep friendships.[16]

Could it be that we were created for more? More than this sick game of comparison and surface conversations?

I don't know about you, but I've had enough.

Enough following the crowd. Enough hashtagging my life away. Enough defining my worth by the number of "likes" I get on Facebook. Enough wasting time trying to fit in. Enough sitting in loneliness and feeling sorry for myself.

I say let's rebel and rediscover what God longs for us to experience in relationships.

Community Is Not a Sunday Service

The desire to connect is in our DNA. God created us in His image—just as He is relational at the core, we too long to be known, loved, valued, and appreciated for who we are. That's why, in all of life, there is nothing more satisfying than deep, meaningful relationships.

The I-can-do-this-on-my-own mind-set is a sham. Just ask the millionaire who traded his marriage and kids for financial success. Or the famous celebrity who has a huge following of fans but no real community of friends. At the end of the day, they will both tell you *it's not worth it.*

> As women, we crave relationships because we need them.

As women, we crave relationships because we need them. Just like we need oxygen. And I'm not talking romantic relationships here. We need godly women in our lives. A safe place to let our hair down. To vent. Laugh. Cry. Scream. Talk. Just sit together. Whatever.

Have you ever had a friend who truly listened, cared, and was there for you? A teacher or mentor who invested in you and spoke truth into your life? A community of people who had your back—who were there for you when your entire world was falling apart?

Chances are, you never forgot it. It changed and shaped who you are today.

And you also know that texting and Facebook messaging are a far cry from the deep emotional and spiritual connection you felt. Because a true friend is the person who walks in when everyone else is walking out.

There's only one thing for sure in this life, Jesus reminds us. "In this world you will have trouble" (John 16:33 NIV). Not very encouraging, I know. But it's the reality of living in a broken, sinful world. And this is precisely why we as women desperately need community. Not just some gals to go shopping with (though I'm all for that!) or chat with on Sunday morning, but also women we can share the deep secrets of our hearts with. Our failures. Worries. Fears. Dreams.

We need each other to survive. To not lose faith. To hold each other accountable. To believe for one another. To be there in the darkest moments of life—and the times of celebration too.

"Let us consider how we may spur one another on toward love and good deeds," Scripture challenges us, "not giving up meeting together, as some are in the habit of doing, but encouraging one another" (Hebrews 10:24–25 NIV).

This is far more serious than just a social club. Or a Sunday morning service. The kind of community God's talking about here is vital to our spiritual and emotional health, regardless of whether we're an introvert or extrovert.

Throughout Scripture, the phrase "one another" and "each other" pops up again and again. Here are just a few examples:

- Comfort one another (1 Thessalonians 4:18 NASB).
- Forgive one another (Colossians 3:13 NIV).
- Build one another up (1 Thessalonians 5:11 ESV).

- Serve one another (Galatians 5:13 NIV).
- Bear one another's burdens (Galatians 6:2 ESV).
- Be kind to one another, tenderhearted, forgiving one another (Ephesians 4:32 ESV).
- Honor one another (Romans 12:10 NIV).
- Care for one another (1 Corinthians 12:25 NASB).
- Minister one to another (1 Peter 4:10 KJV).
- Show hospitality to one another (1 Peter 4:9 ESV).
- Pray for one another (James 5:16 NASB).

God's Word urges us to be there for each other, not just look out for ourselves. And this flies in the face of our *I, me, my* culture. It challenges our busyness that leaves little time to sit and talk with the people we love. To value them with our time and attention.

> It's not just the quantity of Facebook friends that matters but the quality of our actual face-to-face relationships.

Perhaps, then, it's not just the quantity of Facebook friends that matters but the quality of our actual face-to-face relationships.

Could it be that, as Shauna Niequist points out, the best things in life can't be fully expressed in a status update?[17]

Real life is messy. There's no artsy filter to hide our imperfections. And we can't build intimate friendships with five-hundred-plus Facebook friends. So we'll have to be choosy . . . and choose wisely.

My dad often reminds me, "You are who you spend time with," and it's true. *Do I just want to stay safe in my interactions with other people,* I often ask myself, *or do I want to take risks that fundamentally change and shape me as a woman?* The risk to be vulnerable. To let other people in. To seek out mentors. To dare to let my true feelings out in more than an emoticon.

What about you?

One Radical Woman

Imagine it. The economy tanks. There's a food shortage. And your husband dies. Not exactly a fairy-tale ending. #tragedy #wheredoyougofromhere #lifesnotfair

As a young widow, Ruth was faced with a heart-wrenching choice. To move back home and hopefully find another husband, or journey . . . to a country where she'd never been. To say good-bye to Naomi—possibly for good—or leave everything familiar behind.

I can't imagine what an emotional wreck I'd be!

Unlike some mother-in-law relationships, Ruth and Naomi had grown to be very close friends over the years. And the tragedy of both of them losing their husbands only strengthened that bond.

Both women were in a desperate place. No husband. No protection. No support. Only Ruth, as a young woman, could likely remarry and find a new life, while Naomi faced a future of poverty and loneliness.

Shouldering her belongings, Ruth chose the dusty road. Rather than mope and complain, she reached out in love and support to Naomi.

She offered to go with Naomi—that way neither of them would be alone. Together, she said, she and Naomi would make a new life in Bethlehem, and God would be with them.

It seemed so final as they passed through the streets of Moab one last time. Each painful step brought back memories. The familiar marketplace. The courtyard where Ruth had been married to her beloved Mahlon. Laughter. Celebration. Family dinners. All snatched away in an instant.

The men they loved the most were gone.

As the hot afternoon sun beat down on them, Naomi suddenly stopped in her tracks. Her eyes communicated one thing: *You can't do this, Ruth. You can't sacrifice everything—leave everything—for me.*

"Go back. Go home," Naomi tearfully urged. "And may GOD treat you as graciously as you treated . . . me. May GOD give . . . you a new home and a new husband!"

When Ruth felt Naomi's kiss on her cheek, she couldn't hold back the tears any longer. She insisted on going with Naomi.

"Why would you come with me?" Naomi wiped away Ruth's tears. "I'm too old to get a husband. . . . This is a bitter pill for me to swallow—more bitter for me than for you. GOD has dealt me a hard blow."

In that moment, Ruth felt alone—so desperately alone. Confused. Forgotten by God. *If only my husband was here, he would know exactly what to do.*

It was a battle between fear and loyalty.

Fear of the unknown. Fear that she would never find a husband in the land of Judah. As a foreigner, she would likely be viewed as little more than a servant. *Don't I deserve more? Don't I deserve to be loved and cared for too?*

> It was a battle between fear and loyalty. . . . But loyalty won out.

But loyalty won out. Ruth had a deep, heartfelt love for Naomi, her mother-in-law, who had become so dear to her. *I cannot abandon her. I will not. We will face this together, or not at all.*

"Don't force me to leave you," Ruth begged, "don't make me go home. Where you go, I go; and where you live, I'll live. Your people are my people, your God is my god; where you die, I'll die, and that's where I'll be buried, so help me GOD—not even death itself is going to come between us!"

Wow. Talk about a true friend!

In Bethlehem, the barley harvest was just beginning. And Ruth didn't waste any time feeling sorry for herself. She had promised to help provide for Naomi, who was old and feeble.

"I'm going to work," she told Naomi. "I'm going out to glean among the sheaves, following after some harvester who will treat me kindly."

And work she did. By late morning, her legs were itching like crazy. Her back began to ache from leaning over. The hot sun sapped her energy. Her mouth was parched and dry.

Is it really worth it, leaving everything for this? Ruth wanted to cry. Her heart ached with loneliness. No one cared. No one understood.

Or so it seemed. But God saw Ruth's faithfulness and diligence. And so did the big guy in town, Boaz.

He walked toward her, and her heart skipped a beat. Boaz was a very handsome man—the owner of the field. His presence was intimidating, but his eyes were soft and kind.

"Don't go to any other field to glean," he told Ruth. "Stay right here in this one. And stay close to my young women. Watch where they are harvesting and follow them. And don't worry about a thing; I've given orders to my servants not to harass you. When you get thirsty, feel free to go and drink from the water buckets that the servants have filled."

Overwhelmed, Ruth stumbled over her words. "How does this happen that you should pick me out and treat me so kindly—*me*, a foreigner?"

Boaz laughed—a deep, hearty laugh. And his face shone with care. "I've heard all about you—heard about the way you treated your mother-in-law after the death of her husband, and how you left your father and mother and the land of your birth and have come to live among a bunch of total strangers. GOD reward you well for what you've done."

At lunch, Boaz invited Ruth over to eat with the crew. He was intrigued by this woman—he couldn't get her out of his mind. She was beautiful, sure, but what really caught his eye were her caring heart and sacrificial commitment to Naomi.

As she headed back into the field, she overheard Boaz telling the guy in charge, "Pull some of the good stuff out and leave it for her to glean. Give her special treatment."

She was amazed. Grateful. And humbled.

With a skip in her step, Ruth lugged her sack of barley home at the end of the day. She was exhausted—muscles she didn't even know she *had* were aching! But joy danced across her face as she gave Naomi a full report.

"Why, GOD bless that man!" Naomi said. "GOD hasn't quite walked out on us after all! He still loves us, in bad times as well as good! . . . That man, Ruth, is one of our circle of covenant redeemers, a close relative of ours!"

One thing led to another, and Boaz asked Ruth to be his wife. "Don't you worry about a thing; I'll do all you could want or ask. Everybody in town knows what a courageous woman you are—a real prize!"

Don't worry. Ruth's mind drifted back to the battle between fear and loyalty—between Moab and Judah. She had felt so desperately alone. Confused. Forgotten by God.

Yet loyalty to her friend Naomi had won out.

Imagine what would have happened if I had stayed in Moab— stayed where it was comfortable. If I had chosen to go find myself a husband rather than care for Naomi.

Their wedding day was surreal. Ruth pinched herself a million times. "That girl from Moab" everyone had whispered about? She was now the wife of the big guy in town.

God blessed Boaz and Ruth with a son, and the city was abuzz with the news.

"Blessed be GOD!" the townswomen said to Naomi, the proud grandmother. "He didn't leave you without family to carry on your life. . . . And this daughter-in-law who has brought him into the world and loves you so much, why, she's worth more to you than seven sons!"

Ruth. Just an ordinary girl from Moab—who stepped out to do something radical.

As a young widow, Ruth rebelled against everything that made sense, against the look-out-for-number-one mentality the world brainwashes us with. She chose her relationship with Naomi over the promise of a secure future.

She willingly left everything familiar to support and be there for a friend she loved. That's the kind of friend I want to have . . . the kind of woman I want to be!

Ruth and Naomi were there for each other through thick and thin.[18] I wonder how either of them would have fared alone.

Or how we'll fare if we try to live life solo.

True Friends in a Fake World

Let's be honest—we women can be the worst at gossiping. Backbiting. Cliques. Catty arguments. Anything but the "one anothers" that Scripture talks about!

Maybe you're saying, "Megan, that all sounds well and good for Ruth and Naomi, but you don't understand my life. I'm the weird one. No one wants to be my friend. They're nice to my face, but behind my back, they tear me down and make fun of me. I always feel like I'm on the fringe."

Who hasn't been there?

People move. Get married. Take new jobs. In today's transient culture, it's hard to build deep, meaningful relationships. Along the way, we've all been hurt, betrayed, or gossiped about. Maybe it was the popular crowd in high school or your best friend who turned on you. And it only reinforces the American mind-set of individualism.

So we stop relying on others. We shut down. We build walls. We stop appreciating and enjoying the unique plan God has for our lives. Comparison steals our joy, and we begin to morph. We change ourselves—in any way we can—to fit in.

And while we may Instagram our life for the world, we hold people at arm's length. We tell ourselves, *I've got this. I've got a plan . . . and dreams . . . and I'm not going to let anyone get in the way. I can do this on my own. I'll show them.* The only problem is, no matter how much we accomplish, we can't shake the nagging emptiness.

The dissatisfaction of shallow, meaningless conversation. The loneliness we feel, lying in bed at night staring at the ceiling. Wondering what went wrong.

One day back in college, I found a pink sticky note on my desk, left by my mentor. I'd been nursing the wound of a friend who let me down and was having serious doubts about whether relationships were worth it.

Until I read these words by C. S. Lewis:

> There is no safe investment. To love at all is to be vulnerable. Love anything, and your heart will

certainly be wrung and possibly be broken. If you want to make sure of keeping it intact, you must give your heart to no one, not even to an animal. Wrap it carefully round with hobbies and little luxuries; avoid all entanglements; lock it up safe in the casket or coffin of your selfishness. But in that casket—safe, dark, motionless, airless—it will change. It will not be broken; it will become unbreakable, impenetrable, irredeemable.[19]

In that moment I saw through the lie—and I hope you do too. Sure, relationships are hard work. And yes, when we're hurt, betrayed, or taken advantage of, it's easy to go on the defensive. To be skeptical.

But in the end, God created us for relationships—and He didn't specify that we'd get perfect friends. Sometimes, we have to fight through past hurt to open up and trust again. Because, in the body of Christ, it's all about relationships. More than any other influence in all of life, God uses people to shape, grow, and challenge us.

> God uses people to shape, grow, and challenge us.

"Everything God has woven into the fabric of His kingdom promotes interdependence, not individualism," Henry and Richard Blackaby point out.[20] And they're right.

Where our culture values toughness and independence, we've got to rebel. Because we see through the lie. We know that putting up a false front leads only to loneliness and pity parties. So we've got to take risks to be honest. To let other people in.

Where peer pressure threatens to negatively shape us, we've got to rebel. We know that God created us to live in community where we're known and loved for exactly who we are. So we have to seek out godly friends and mentors. People who push us toward God, not pull us away.

There's an old African proverb that says, "If you want to go fast, go alone. If you want to go far, go together."

We need each other, and we need a new culture that values honesty, vulnerability, weakness, and interdependence. We were meant to share life face-to-face—to pray for and support one another, not just comment on each other's Facebook statuses.

It's time to stop comparing. Stop the gossiping. Stop the fake smiles and the shallow conversations. It's all a sham that leaves us empty.

Let's start connecting. Let's dare to trust. Let's stop just "liking" statuses and start doing life together. Let's be the body of Christ for each other—in moments of celebration as well as in times of tragedy and loss.

> Let's stop just "liking" statuses and start doing life together.

Let's wrap our arms—and our hearts—around one another, to create a safe haven that weathers the storms of life.

Because, in the end, it's not ultimately about winning a gold medal or catching Boaz's eye. It's about building a community that is radically different.

Ann Voskamp points this out: "Girls rival each other. Women *revive* each other. Girls empale each other. Women *empower* each other. Girls compare each other. Women *champion* each other."[21]

Oh, that we would rise up to be women—not just girls! And maybe, just maybe, a world that is aching with loneliness will stop and take notice.

"This is how everyone will recognize that you are my disciples—when they see the love you have for each other" (John 13:35).

Someone has to step out and take the risk to be a woman of God, not just another petty girl. Will you?

CHAPTER EIGHT

Something to Live For

Don't ask yourself what the world needs.
Ask yourself what makes you come alive and
then go do that. Because what the world
needs is people who have come alive.

—*Howard Thurman*

O KAY, God, YOU PICKED THE WRONG PERSON."[1] The words slipped out of eighteen-year-old Katie's mouth as she looked out over 140 squirming kids cramped in a tiny barn-turned-schoolhouse in a small Ugandan village.

Homecoming queen. Class president. A GPA to boast about. Katie Davis was on the track to success. As a competitive high school senior, she could name a college and go almost anywhere.

But a three-week mission trip to Uganda changed everything. For the first time in her life, Katie came face-to-face with real poverty.

Thirty million people. Half of the nation's population was children. Many orphaned by AIDS. Living on less than a dollar a day.[2]

Children who wake up every morning with the gnawing pangs of hunger. Become sick because of malnourishment and poor nutrition. Dig through trash to find something—anything—to eat. Fight just to stay alive.

Coming from a comfortable life growing up in Tennessee, Katie was aghast. "I was so overwhelmed by this need . . . unlike any kind of poverty I had ever experienced."[3]

Yet Katie was also shocked to find surprising joy. Working among people who had *nothing*, she saw smiles everywhere. Laughter. Giving. Sharing. Contentment. Gratitude. Genuine love.

Walking the dusty roads of Uganda, Katie Davis found Jesus like never before. And it began to radically change her. She says, "I fell more in love with Him, and He stripped me of the things that I had relied on."[4]

Back home in Tennessee, Katie couldn't get Uganda out of her mind. Beautiful people. Desperate eyes. Children wasting away. "I didn't know what I would do about it, but I knew I had to do something."[5]

After finishing high school, Katie returned to teach kindergarten in a small Ugandan village, thinking, *I'll take this year off, do this missions thing . . . and then I'll come back, go to college, and have a normal life.*

It was an ordinary January day, until Katie got the news that her neighbor's house had collapsed and a little girl had been injured.

Rushing to the medical clinic, Katie's heart went out to nine-year-old Agnes, who lay in the hospital bed nearly unconscious.

She was equally shocked when the medical staff refused to help. Why? There was no one to pay the bill. Agnes had lost her parents years earlier, and she had been helping her grandmother raise her seven- and five-year-old siblings since then.

"Do whatever you need to do," Katie told the doctor. "I'll figure out a way to pay for it."[6] Not only was Agnes injured but she was also now homeless. Along with her two younger sisters, Mary and Scovia.

Katie didn't know where to get the money—or how exactly to help—but she stepped out in faith that God would provide.

"It seemed obvious to me," Katie remembers. "They didn't have a place to stay—I had a house."[7]

She invited the girls to stay with her until they figured out where they could go.

Katie searched for a living family member—an aunt, uncle, or grandparent who could take in these precious girls. But she found no one.

A few days later, five-year-old Scovia looked up to Katie. Her one word changed everything.

"Mommy?"

With that word, something clicked in Katie's heart. She sensed God telling her, *You are the family for these girls that you are looking for.* [8]

"Adoption entered my world before I even knew it was called that," Katie says, looking back now.[9] Within the year, Katie's little family continued to grow . . . and grow . . . as she welcomed eight Ugandan girls who had no family.

Katie also sought to help empower local families with resources to make it possible for children to continue to live with their parents rather than being placed in foster care or an orphanage. And she quickly realized that she couldn't do it alone. Calling and e-mailing family and friends back home, she asked them to consider donating money to help cover the cost of school fees for many of the children, who would otherwise be forced to work, beg . . . or worse. "Ten sponsors turned to forty. Forty turned to a hundred . . . and Amazima Ministries was born."[10] *Amazima* means "truth" in the local language, and Katie's heart is just that.

And the take-a-year-off-before-college-and-do-this-missions-thing plan? *About that.* Katie came back to the US after she finished her year of teaching kindergarten, but she was unsettled. Dissatisfied. Torn.

Well-meaning friends and family members were skeptical. After all, she dare not pass up college scholarships and getting started with her career.

College? Career? My heart is in Uganda—with my little girls.

After almost caving, Katie said, "It felt like turning my back on what God was trying to do in my life, and that's a horrible feeling."[11]

Uganda wasn't just a yearlong trip. It's a lifetime journey, Katie realized.

As she sought God, Katie began to take His commands more seriously than ever before.

No excuses. No exceptions. No holding back. And it changed everything.

Katie fought through the lies of comfort, safety, and self-satisfaction—and her own parents' expectations—to find the truth of God's heart for the world.

After a one-way ticket back to Uganda, Katie has no regrets. Now the mother of thirteen children, this young woman is daring to live out the biblical command to "look after orphans and widows" (James 1:27 NIV).

"Love is not about numbers," Katie shares. "Love is about real people."[12]

Agnes is not just a statistic.

"She is a real person. She is my daughter. And she is God's child."[13]

Katie works among the poorest of the poor in the slums of Masese, teaching women vocational skills so they don't have to turn to prostitution to support their families.

These days, the locals joke that Katie's house is Grand Central Station. "There's no telling who you'll find there," she laughs. "Someone who needs a glass of water. Someone who needs a meal. Someone who needs medical care. Someone who needs advice. Someone who needs prayer.

"It's amazing to see what God can do when we just open our doors."[14]

From street children to homeless families, alcoholics to prostitutes, Katie refuses to let fear or prejudice hold her back.

"I have learned that I will not change the world. Jesus will do that. I can, however, change the world for one person. I can change the world for thirteen little girls and for four hundred school children and for a sick and dying grandmother and for a malnourished, neglected, abused five-year-old."[15]

Katie gets it. She is a rebel at heart.

She is rebelling against the lie of the American Dream—that life is all about getting. About being comfortable and having fun. About making lots of money and finding a man and buying a lot of nice things.

She is rebelling against the lie that she can't make a difference. That God can't use her as a single woman. That she's too young. Too inexperienced.

Instead, Katie dares to believe. To really take God at His word and actually live it out, putting feet to her faith. Whether she's teaching her kids, tending wounds, or sitting by the bedside of a dying AIDS patient.

She spends her life with "the least of these" (Matthew 25:40 NIV).

This young woman fights through doubt and insecurity to trust God. And steps out into the slums in obedience to Him every single day.

A lot of people consider Katie courageous or radical, but she'd be the first to disagree. "I am really not that brave, I am not really that strong, and I am not doing anything spectacular. I am just doing what God called me to do as a follower of Him. Feed His sheep, do unto the least of His people."[16]

She admits, "There are days that it is so overwhelming—the poverty and the devastation. There are days when I wonder what the point is of saving one child if you can't save them all. But Jesus is calling me to come."[17]

She adds, "If one person sees the love of Christ in me, it is worth every minute. In fact, it is worth spending my life for."[18]

Katie Davis is just an ordinary girl from Tennessee who says yes to God—every single day. And it makes me wonder.

What does God long to do through you and me to change our world?

The Perfect Plan ... Gone Wrong

A sprawling house. The husband of my dreams. Two kids—a boy and a girl. A Suburban in the driveway. Competitive careers. Money in the bank. A big backyard ... and oh, did I mention the white picket fence?

It's easy to get sucked in to the American Dream. From TV to movies to music stars, everything in our culture screams that life is all about success. Making a name for ourselves.

Status. Power. Fame. Climbing to the top. And having fun along the way.

As twenty-somethings, we're programmed to value education, career advancement, and building a secure financial future. That's code for being rich.

Money, money, money.

It's not surprising, then, that 75 percent of today's college students say being wealthy is very important to them.[19]

We've been criticized for being entitled. Self-absorbed. Overly confident. Focused more on our Facebook status and designer outfit than on making a meaningful difference in the world.

In a recent article title, *Time* magazine dubbed millennials the "Me Me Me Generation."[20]

Ouch. We hate to admit that it's true. Many of us are taking our time growing up. And between the hangovers and hookups, we're searching for something more. *More money? A better job? Maybe that's the answer.*

As we stare at an average debt of thirty-five thousand dollars in student loans and are faced with the reality that fewer than half of us land a career job, disillusionment creeps in. A sinking feeling that we've been gypped.

What if there's more?

More than designer clothes. Gucci handbags. A daily Starbucks trip. Vacations to the Bahamas. A cell phone upgrade every six months. An iPod. And an iPad. And whatever comes next.

We've watched our parents chase after the American Dream. And they're still chasing, running faster than ever in today's struggling economy.

It's a never-ending quest for self-fulfillment. And many of us are skeptical. So we respond in one of two ways—as Peter Panners or Wall Street Wannabes.

Peter Panners. Some of us take Peter Pan's advice to heart and make a pact with our friends never to grow up. Rebelling against the American Dream, we try to re-create the college dorm room lifestyle—only, wait, we're not seventeen anymore; we're twenty-seven.

We fight maturity. We drag our feet. We drift through life. But, boy, we're having a lot of fun along the way.

"Life is all about me . . . What I want. When I want it. How I want it. With whomever I want. And nobody is gonna tell me what to do." That's the rallying cry of the Peter Pan culture.

Wall Street Wannabes. Then there are those of us who are a bit more mature, we think. We're achievers who buck the tide of widespread immaturity and actually begin the hard work of growing up.

Working a job—or two, or three. Paying bills. Saving money.

We couldn't care less about partying, but we are quickly consumed with status. Appearance. Getting in good with the boss. Building our résumé. One rung at a time, we're climbing to the top.

Youthful ambition paves the road to the "self-made woman." But our accomplishments go to our heads, and eventually we stop seeing and valuing people. We stop connecting. So we use people to get what we want. Relationships become dispensable, and we're willing to step on anyone we need to along the way.

The downside of the American Dream, says one commentator, is that people tend to pursue success at any cost, which ends up destroying the dream.[21]

Following the good (or not-so-good) example of our parents, Wall Street Wannabes are intent on building "the good life"—with one difference. Whatever our parents did, we do *more of.* Wall Street Wannabes are intent on making sure we escape the frustrating rat race we are caught in so one day we can actually enjoy life.

But at what cost? Our relationships? Health? Life satisfaction? Only time will tell.

Wherever you are, I want to ask you to do something radical. Stop—for just a moment—and consider, *Was I made for something more?* More than partying with the Peter Panners or breaking your back with the Wall Street Wannabes?

The American Dream is killing us inside. It's shallow. Empty. Unsatisfying. And we can never get enough. Could there be something more?

I Have a Dream

Piercing brown eyes. One of the most engaging smiles I've ever seen. A dirt floor. And four days in Nicaragua that would change my life forever.

Her name was Reyna. Her picture had been on my refrigerator for years. Morning after morning, I would pause to pray for this precious little girl while I drank my coffee.

Growing up, my family always set money aside to support kids whose parents couldn't. Reyna was one of those children, and now I was meeting her face-to-face.

Sitting on a makeshift bench in Reyna's tiny house, I noticed a line of white papers taped to the wall. Thinking it was the newspaper, I leaned in closer.

No . . . they're letters. Letters our family had written to Reyna over the years. Reminders that God loves her and that she hasn't been forgotten. That there is hope—even though her dad died and her mom was struggling to put food on the table.

Reyna sidled up next to me and reached up to pull my face down next to hers. "I love you, sister," she whispered in Spanish, planting a big wet kiss on my cheek.

Tears sprang to my eyes as I began to realize the full weight of my relationship with this little girl. The opportunity to go to school, and new shoes to walk there every day. Knowing there would be food on the table when she got home. No longer begging for food.

Even though I don't have a daughter yet—in a way, I really do.

And it all started with thirty dollars—a seemingly insignificant amount in my world. Thirty dollars a month I could have spent at Starbucks. To shop at the mall. Or to grab dinner out with my girlfriends.

Thirty dollars a month that I chose not to spend on myself but instead to give to Reyna's family. It changed everything.

Now, as I sip my coffee in the morning and pray for Reyna, I'm reminded that money and stuff get old after a while. You can fit only so many clothes in your closet. The excitement of new shoes or yet another handbag eventually fades.

And I've got to tell you, it's nothing compared to the joy of investing in someone else's life. Watching God work through you to bring life out of death. Hope out of desperation. Transformation. Healing. And a future.

It's thrilling. Seriously.

I don't want to waste my life on stuff that doesn't matter. To rebel and follow God, we've got to ask ourselves, *Are we throwing away precious time pursuing things that don't really matter?*

> To rebel and follow God, we've got to ask ourselves, *Are we throwing away precious time pursuing things that don't really matter?*

Compared to the rest of the world, most of us have grown up with a silver spoon in our mouths. Never worrying about a roof over our heads. Or walking barefoot to school in the snow. Never living in fear of being captured by a guerrilla army. Or tempted to sell our bodies for sex so we could have food.

We take *so much* for granted. To be honest, we don't really have a clue what it's like to be in need.

It's time we open our eyes.

It's time we step out of our comfortable Christian cocoon and actually see orphans, widows, slaves, HIV/AIDS victims, and the poor not as statistics but as real people. People who desperately need to experience God's love, grace, and hope. Through us.

This is the true dream of a lifetime—to live like Jesus, whether it's in Virginia, California, Uganda, or Nicaragua. Stop and think about it. Jesus spent the majority of His time with the poor. Outcasts. Prostitutes. Tax collectors. The down-and-outers.

Sure, Hollywood stars give money to help orphans in Africa. So do Mark Zuckerberg and Britney Spears. Our generation cares about social justice and humanitarian aid—and that's great. But for many, it's just a "project."

It can quickly become about trendy T-shirts, the latest brace-let campaign, and showing everyone how "cool" we are. It's easy to talk big. To say we love God but live like the world. We may give a little money or take a short-term trip, but our lives still center on being comfortable, safe, happy, and having fun.

Jesus asks for more.

He's not just asking for your tithe. He's asking for your heart. Your life. Your dreams and ambitions. He's asking for everything.

"Knowing the correct password—saying 'Master, Master,' for instance—isn't going to get you anywhere with me," Jesus told His disciples . . . and us. "What is required is serious obedi-ence—*doing* what my Father wills. I can see it now—at the Final Judgment thousands strutting up to me and saying, 'Master, we preached the Message, we bashed the demons, our God-sponsored projects had everyone talking.' And do you know what I am going to say? 'You missed the boat. All you did was use me to make yourselves important. You don't impress me one bit. You're out of here'" (Matthew 7:21–23).

God-sponsored projects. I'm guilty of that. We've got to check our hearts here. Are we using God, Christianity, or even mission work to make ourselves look important? To brag about what we're doing for God? Is our service to others really about being visible and noticed? Showing everyone else that we're "good Christians"?

Even in Christian circles, we've watered down "missions" and lost God's heart. But building God's kingdom isn't necessarily about going to another country. And living missionally doesn't mean getting people to pray a prayer; it's a lifestyle of sacrifice, service, and love.

> Living missionally doesn't mean getting people to pray a prayer; it's a lifestyle of sacrifice, service, and love.

Living with less, so we can be the hands and feet of Jesus— giving of our time, our money, and our energy. Loving the orphan. Serving the widow. Investing in people the rest of the world has forgotten. Sharing the truth of the gospel through our words and our actions.

"It may take place in a foreign land or it may take place in your backyard," Katie Davis challenges us, "but I believe that we were each created to change the world for *someone*. To serve *someone*. To love *someone* the way Christ first loved us, to spread His light. This is the dream, and it is possible."[22]

Jesus' entire ministry was centered on loving and serving and giving. It was His heartbeat—the heartbeat of the gospel.

"For God so *loved* the world that he gave his one and only Son" (John 3:16 NIV; emphasis added). "The Son of Man did not come to be served, but to serve, and to give his life as a ransom for many" (Mark 10:45 NIV).

If we dare to call ourselves Christ-followers, this must be our heartbeat as well. It must influence our friendships. Our attitudes about work. How we spend our free time. And our money. What we choose to do without. How we treat strangers. How we respond to the homeless guy on the side of the road. And how we love the difficult people in our life.

What could be said of you?

"Megan so loved herself that she gave nothing . . ." or "Megan so loved those in her world that she gave *everything* . . ."

> I have a dream that this generation will cast aside the shallow promises of the American Dream and instead say yes to God—with our whole hearts.

Everything. I have a dream that this generation will cast aside the shallow promises of the American Dream and instead say yes to God—with our whole hearts.

That we'll stop wasting our time building our own little kingdoms and instead give our lives to building God's kingdom.

That we'll stop trying to create a posh life for ourselves and instead fully surrender.

Just like one woman in ancient Palestine.

One Radical Woman

Remember your life as a thirteen-year-old? Best friends. Sleepovers. Passing notes in class. Your first crush. Dreaming about the future. And the emotional roller coaster we call adolescence.

She was a peasant girl in a remote village. Young. Poor. A nobody.

But God took notice. He saw her pure heart. Her love for Yahweh. Her humility and willingness to say yes. Her incredible trust in His plan.

That's my girl! He smiled, looking over at Gabriel with a sparkle in His eyes.

So Gabriel spread his wings and took flight. Destination: Nazareth.

Mary rubbed the sleep out of her eyes as the sun rose over Galilee. Roosters crowing in the distance. Children laughing. Mothers scolding. The street outside her window coming to life as people made their way to the market. To the well. To the village square.

All under the watchful eye of Roman guards.

But young Mary was caught up daydreaming. A smile danced across her face as she thought about Joseph. Her betrothed. He was respected and loved by all who knew him. He was a descendant of King David himself.

And he was her future husband.

What will our future look like together? Mary wondered, watching the neighbor kids chase each other down the street. *Will God bless us with children?*

"Good morning!" Mary jumped at the booming voice behind her. Turning around, her breath caught in her throat. She fell to the ground terrified.

It was some kind of heavenly being. His glowing presence filled the entire house. And the light—it was blinding.

This is the end. I'm going to die. Panic filled her racing heart.

"You're beautiful with God's beauty," Gabriel continued. "Beautiful inside and out! God be with you."

A strange mix of confusion, fear, and curiosity washed over Mary. *What on earth? Me . . . beautiful? I'm just an ordinary girl.*

It was as if he saw right through her. Gabriel knew.

"Mary, you have nothing to fear."

He knows my name?

"God has a surprise for you: You will become pregnant and give birth to a son and call his name Jesus."

This is so weird—an angel telling me I'm going to have a baby?

"He will be great," Gabriel continued, "be called 'Son of the Highest.' The Lord God will give him the throne of his father David; he will rule Jacob's house forever—no end, ever, to his kingdom."

Son of the Most High? A king who would reign forever? Mary tried to make sense of it all. *Me . . . have a baby . . . now? It's impossible.*

Gabriel talked like it was the most logical thing in the world.

"But how?" her words tumbled out. "I've never slept with a man."

"The Holy Spirit will come upon you, the power of the Highest hover over you. Therefore, the child you bring to birth will be called Holy, Son of God."

God's Son! The Messiah? Growing inside of me? Maybe it was all a dream.

But Gabriel continued. "Did you know that your cousin Elizabeth conceived a son, old as she is? Everyone called her barren, and here she is six months pregnant! Nothing, you see, is impossible with God."

How am I supposed to explain this to my parents? To Joseph? What if no one believes me? To have a baby without being married—it will be a disgrace to everyone.

A thousand images flooded Mary's mind. She envisioned her friends turning a cold shoulder. Crossing over to the other side of the street to avoid her. Whispering. Laughing.

Whore. Sleazy. Loose. She would be shunned. No one would understand.

Her parents weeping. Disappointed. Hurt.

And Joseph, her beloved. How would he respond? Would he divorce her? Leave her all alone—like everyone else surely would? She would be an unwed mother.

Yet in an instant, Gabriel's confident words cut through it all. "Nothing . . . is impossible with God."

Yahweh. The God I've learned about since I was a little girl. This message is from Him? The God who parted the Red Sea to bring our forefathers out of Egypt. Who destroyed Pharaoh's army in its waters. The God who provided manna in the wilderness. Who brought water out of a rock.

The God who has promised to bring us a deliverer. The Messiah.

Why me, God? Out of all the girls in Israel, why did you choose me?

Mary was overwhelmed. Humbled. Honored. Terrified.

And, in that moment, she had a choice—to laugh it off as a bad dream or to say yes.

She could have told Gabriel, *It's too hard. It's too scary. It's too uncomfortable. You don't understand. People will hate me. Joseph will break up with me. And I'm not ready to be a single mom. I'll be the laughingstock of town. I have no way to provide for a baby—I'm just a girl. I'm thirteen years old, for crying out loud! Tell God to go find someone else.*

But no. Mary rebelled against the fear. The need to understand and make sense of it all. She rebelled against everything in her that wanted to stay safe. Comfortable. And silent.

Instead, Mary made the gutsy choice to say yes.

"I'm the Lord's maid, ready to serve," she replied, her voice wavering. "Let it be with me just as you say."

And just like that, the angel was gone. *Poof.* And Mary was once again alone in the room. The laughter of children filtered in through the window. The chatter of women on the way to the well. The distant shouts of neighbors, herding cattle. The warm sun on her face.

Mary instinctively reached down and touched her stomach. *Could it be true?*

Her emotions said no, and her mind said, "This is crazy," but she willed her attention back to the truths she'd known since she was a little girl.

I don't understand—it still seems impossible to me—but I choose to trust Yahweh. If this angel is really from Him, I know that He can do anything. Anything. He will provide for me and protect me. He will not leave me alone.

Elizabeth—she would understand. Mary didn't waste any time going to visit her cousin.

Her cousin greeted her at the door, and . . . the angel was right! Elizabeth was definitely pregnant, her stomach round as a giant pomegranate. Mary nearly laughed at the sight. So it was true!

"You're so blessed among women, and the babe in your womb, also blessed!" Elizabeth was giddy with excitement.

"Why am I so blessed that the mother of my Lord visits me?" Elizabeth continued. "The moment the sound of your greeting entered my ears, the babe in my womb skipped like a lamb for sheer joy. Blessed woman, who believed what God said, believed every word would come true!"

She knows? Of course she knows . . . God must have told her too. Mary's heart welled up with emotion. Joy replaced fear. Excitement replaced anxiety. And assurance took the place of worry . . . assurance of God's promises.

It was as if God whispered, *I've got this, Mary. I'll walk with you each step of the way. Just trust Me, and watch Me work a miracle that will change the entire world.*

A song broke forth from Mary's heart:

I'm bursting with God-news;
   I'm dancing the song of my Savior God.
God took one good look at me, and look what happened—
   I'm the most fortunate woman on earth!
What God has done for me will never be forgotten,
   the God whose very name is holy, set apart from all others.
His mercy flows in wave after wave
   on those who are in awe before him.

In wave after wave, God's mercy flowed over Mary's life. Joseph stood by her, thanks to an angel messenger God sent. Strangers provided shelter from the cold as Mary gave birth to the promised Child. Again, an angel warned the young couple of soldiers coming to kill Jesus, and the little family fled to Egypt.

And all this before she was fifteen years old! Can you imagine?

Mary watched Jesus grow from a toddling infant to a strapping young boy to a full-grown man. Her heart swelled with pride and wonder as she watched Jesus work. Healing the sick. Making the blind see. Confronting the Pharisees. Even bringing the dead back to life. His teachings were radical. Refreshing. And crowds followed Him.

What will happen to Him, Lord? The Roman government was becoming more oppressive by the day—crushing anyone they viewed as a threat.

Standing at the foot of the cross, Mary wept. There were no words to describe her agony. *Where are You, God? What about all Your promises?*

"Woman." The voice belonged to Jesus. Struggling to get the words out. Each breath labored. She barely recognized His battered, bleeding body.

"Here is your son." She looked and saw John—one of Jesus' closest friends.

And to John, Jesus whispered, "Here is your mother."

Mary struggled to take it in. Her son's eyes were full of love and compassion that pierced her soul; it seemed as if He was saying, *It's going to be okay. I already know the end of the story. Trust Me.*

Wholehearted trust. Unwavering obedience. That's what characterized Mary's life.

> Mary rebelled against fear and chose faith. She rebelled against the need to control her own life and surrendered to God's plan.

What a radical woman! Mary rebelled against fear and chose faith. She rebelled against the need to control her own life and surrendered to God's plan.[23]

Mary wasn't perfect by any means, but she was 100 percent willing. And God took notice.

"GOD is always on the alert," the Bible tells us, "constantly on the lookout for people who are totally committed to him" (2 Chronicles 16:8).

Our God chooses the most unlikely people. He's not necessarily looking for the rich and powerful to change the world. All He asks for is a willing heart. And obedience wherever He places us.

Change Your World

Find out where God is working and join Him there. Henry and Richard Blackaby give us this challenge in their book *Experiencing God.*[24] It sounds too simple. But seriously, what a radical idea! Our world is all about self-promotion and self-satisfaction. Pursuing our own dreams and goals. Getting what we want in life.

Everything around us screams, "It's all about you! You deserve it!"

But to follow Christ, we have to rebel.

"Anyone who intends to come with me has to let me lead," Jesus says. "You're not in the driver's seat; *I* am" (Matthew 16:24).

Or, as we often read it, "If anyone would come after me, let him deny himself and take up his cross and follow me" (ESV).

Total control—that's what God asks for. He wants us to give Him complete control of our relationships. Our careers. Our friends. Our money. Our sexuality. Our time. Our future.

Even when you're hurting, He is there. So "don't run from suffering," God's Word continues. "Embrace it. Follow me and I'll show you how. Self-help is no help at all. Self-sacrifice is the way, my way, to finding yourself, your true self. What kind of deal is it to get everything you want but lose yourself?" (Matthew 16:25–26).

I don't want to get to the end of my life, stand before God, and have regrets. I don't want to look back and realize, *I woulda . . . coulda . . . shoulda.*

We need a heart shift. We need regular, conscious reminders that direct our attention to what really matters. It's a daily struggle. As the apostle Paul said, "I have the desire to do what is right, but not the ability to carry it out. For I do not do the good I want, but the evil I do not want is what I keep on doing" (Romans 7:18–19 ESV).

That's why we're commanded, "Consider yourselves dead to sin and alive to God in Christ Jesus" (Romans 6:11 ESV).

Before God can work through us, He first has to work in us. Giving up control. Embracing radical trust. Staying connected to Him. Taking life one step at a time—with keen eyes and a willing heart.

Consider Jesus' last words before returning to heaven: "It is not for you to know the times or dates the Father has set by his own authority" (Acts 1:7 NIV).

Release the vise grip on your heart and life.

"But you will receive power when the Holy Spirit comes on you" (v. 8 NIV).

God will empower you for whatever He calls you to.

"And you will be my witnesses in Jerusalem, and in all Judea and Samaria, and to the ends of the earth" (v. 8 NIV).

No matter who you are or what your past is, God can use you. He wants to use you. Whether it's in your own neighborhood or on the other side of the world.

So what's in front of you? What's your "Jerusalem"?

It's easy to romanticize serving God, but we have to check our motives. These days, it's trendy and cool to go on a mission trip to the slums of India or the villages of Uganda. A few weeks of discomfort . . . a "missions high" . . . and back to the comfort of home.

In reality, it's much harder to live missionally in the ordinariness of life. But it's all about starting in the now. Whether it's waiting tables, studying for the next test, or working a job we're not passionate about . . . how do we serve God in our day-to-day life? How do we love the people who annoy us the most? The people who get in the way of our dreams?

It starts in the now. Maybe those people are God's dream for you. Your coworkers who don't know Jesus. The people you interact with every day at the gym. The Muslim family next door who just lost their baby. The single moms in your community who just can't make ends meet. The gangs in your inner city who are desperate for hope. The HIV patients who think God has forgotten them. The family member who drives you up the wall.

"Be obedient in whatever God is putting in front of you," Katie challenges us. "It doesn't always look like moving to another country. . . . But he places a need in front of us . . . and it's our job to obey and meet that need."[25]

It's about your brother. The girl at school nobody talks to. Your neighbors. Your roommate. Your coworkers. God loves to do the extraordinary through the ordinary. Serving others selflessly will break our hearts, change our lives, and draw us into a deeper relationship with God.

It takes radical trust to step out into the unknown. To rebel against a world that constantly tries to seduce us with money and power.

To turn the American Dream on its head and do just the opposite—rather than hoarding, choosing to give until it hurts.

Rather than making a name for ourselves, choosing to serve others from a pure heart.

Rather than always hanging out with people like us, choosing to reach out to those that others poke fun at and dismiss.

Rather than living a comfortable and safe life, choosing to embrace a radical faith and obey God, even when it looks crazy to the people around us.

> Ultimately, it's not about *where* we live so much as *how* we live.

Ultimately, it's not about *where* we live so much as *how* we live.

I'm reminded of my grandpa's favorite verse: "Now it is required that those who have been given a trust must prove faithful" (1 Corinthians 4:2 NIV).

We must be faithful in the little things. Obedient regarding what's in front of us. And leaving the rest to God.

Who knows? God might touch an entire generation through our faithfulness and obedience.

Let's go for it!

God, whatever . . . wherever . . . however You want to use me, I say yes!

CHAPTER NINE

Rebel and Be Set Free

I have one desire now—to live a life of
reckless abandon for the Lord, putting
all my energy and strength into it.

—*Elisabeth Elliot*

N O RESERVES. NO RETREATS. NO REGRETS."
Three simple phrases written in William Borden's Bible.
Heir to the Borden family fortune, William was already roll-
ing in his family's wealth. As a high school graduation present,
William's parents gave him a trip to travel the globe. It was on
this trip that he first saw and was burdened by the dire needs of
those hurting and dying around the world. Upon returning to
the States, William declared his desire to become a missionary.
In response to his friends' backlash about his decision, he wrote
two words in his Bible: "No reserves." William had the world at

his fingertips, yet he chose to invest in the only thing that really matters—people.

During his freshman year at Yale, William started meeting with a buddy every morning to pray and read Scripture. Praying for his classmates to come and know Jesus. By the time William graduated in 1909, one thousand of Yale's thirteen hundred students were meeting in morning prayer groups.

From widows and orphans, to the disabled and homeless, William saw every person as valuable and worth investing in. One friend remembers he "might often be found in the lower parts of the city at night, on the street, in a cheap lodging house or some restaurant to which he had taken a poor hungry fellow to feed him, seeking to lead men to Christ."[1]

William was competitive—and high-paying job offers were coming in left and right. But he turned them down to serve the Muslim Kansu people in China. In his Bible, he wrote two more words: "No retreats."

After finishing his graduate work at Princeton Seminary, William decided to sail for China. Because he was hoping to minister to Muslims, he stopped in Egypt to study Arabic. While there, this fearless young man contracted spinal meningitis. He died within a month.

Twenty-five years old. His life snuffed out prematurely. Was it a tragedy? Or a glorious sacrifice?

"Borden not only gave away his wealth, but himself, in a way so joyous and natural that it seemed a privilege rather than a sacrifice."[2]

William left a legacy in just twenty-five short years of life. After his death, his tattered Bible was found containing one more phrase, penned just below the first two:

"No reserves. No retreats. *No regrets.*"[3]

William Borden was rebellious. He saw through the emptiness of money, power, and worldly success . . . and he chose Jesus.

What about you?

From Kool-Aid . . . to Living Water

Culture is playing with our hearts, our lives, and our futures. It's destroying us from the inside out. The blind are leading the blind en masse.

"For wide is the gate and broad is the road that leads to destruction, and many enter through it" (Matthew 7:13 NIV).

Many? Are you one of those many? Or will you be one of the called-out few? A woman who takes God at His Word? Will you dare to believe and follow Christ in a world that says moral values and integrity are crazy?

> Will you dare to believe and follow Christ in a world that says moral values and integrity are crazy?

Jesus continues, "Small is the gate and narrow the road that leads to life, and only a few find it" (Matthew 7:14 NIV).

Eight percent. According to one recent study, that's the percentage of twenty-somethings who stay "intensely devoted to their faith into young adulthood"—not only attending church but also pursuing a God-centered, God-honoring lifestyle grounded in biblical values.[4]

My heart aches to read these words. Eight percent? So few? It seems almost incomprehensible. And then I remember Jesus' words: "When the Son of Man comes, will he find faith on the earth?" (Luke 18:8 NIV).

> What are you building your life on? Who are you allowing to influence and shape you?

I pray that wherever you find yourself—in the 8 percent or the 92 percent—you'll take a moment to stop and consider. Take stock about your spiritual direction. What are you building your life on? Who are you allowing to influence and shape you?

This could be the moment where everything changes.

You see, this is not a cute Christian book. It's not just about inspirational Bible stories or those special few people who do something "big" for God. It's an invitation for every single one of us—today—to stop drinking the Kool-Aid and instead start drinking the living water from Jesus that "will become in [you] a spring of water welling up to eternal life" (John 4:14 NIV).

This book is the battle cry of one woman who is tired of namby-pamby Christianity. Sure, there's plenty of religion—but little or no power. Little or no heart transformation. Little or no cultural impact. And so we sit and keep quiet while our culture forcefully advances its lies.

God is not calling you and me to be women who are content with simply going to church on Sunday or doing a Bible study. No way! He's looking for rebellious women. Women with burning hearts and unquenched voices. Women who will stand in the gap and speak God's truth.

He is searching for women who will rebel—every single day—against the lies of this world. Lies about how we look. What matters in life. Where our identity is.

God is looking for women who will commit themselves to Him and live free with no reserves, no retreats, and no regrets.

> God is looking for women who will commit themselves to Him and live free with no reserves, no retreats, and no regrets.

Rebels in Real Life

You may feel all alone. Maybe you're surrounded by classmates who mock your faith. Or coworkers who think you are weird and narrow-minded. Maybe no guy in your circle of friends will date you because you're too "uptight" (in other words, you won't have sex with him).

Following God can feel lonely sometimes.

As you rebel against our culture's lies, you are joining women of all ages, from all around the world, who are also courageously stepping up.

But let me assure you: you are not alone. As you rebel against our culture's lies, you are joining women of all ages, from all around the world, who are also courageously stepping up. Remember these gals?

Mo Isom. Mo is a rebel—breaking out of the victim mindset. She dares to believe that God created her for a purpose. That she is more than a girl who screwed up, messed around with boys, and lost her dad to suicide.

Melissa Brock. Melissa is a rebel—challenging herself to see in the mirror the woman that God hand fashioned, not a fat, ugly, good-for-nothing girl. She is a voice of hope for women who battle with self-hatred and eating disorders.

Jen Barrick. Jen is a rebel—taking a stand against hopelessness. She fights to see God working a miracle far greater than physical healing. The miracle of other people finding Jesus through her story.

Teresa Scanlan. Teresa is a rebel—exalting Jesus in a pageant world of self-promotion and cheap beauty. She harnesses the power of her influence to challenge women toward confidence in who God uniquely created them to be.

Lolo Jones. Lolo is a rebel—standing her ground in a world that thinks she's crazy. She doesn't apologize for her biblical moral values or cave in to peer pressure. She is set on honoring God with her sexuality.

Gabby Douglas. Gabby is a rebel—cultivating authentic relationships in a world that's all about the self-made woman. Growing up without a dad, she fought to trust again and let others in. And now she's passionate about giving back, being a role model and a blessing to others.

Katie Davis. Katie is a rebel—breaking the mold of the American Dream to live in a remote Ugandan village. She kicks comfort and safety to the curb to obey God and mother thirteen orphaned girls.

And you. You, too, can rebel against the lies and be a radical woman. No matter what your age. Married or single. No matter what your past failures. Your insecurities. Or your deepest secrets.

So what will your story be? Life is all about choices. Decisions that we make or don't make—and indecision is a decision too.

Will you choose to join the ranks of women who say enough is enough? Or will you spend your life desperately trying the latest fads and values, constantly changing who you are to fit in with a culture that doesn't care about you?

Are you going to look back with regret? Emptiness? Thinking, *I woulda . . . coulda . . . shoulda?*

Or will you dare to take a rebellious, radical step today—and every day—toward Jesus and lifelong change?

#Letsdoit #Berebellious #Startstoday

I beg you—see the world's lies for the empty sham that they are. Let's not be women who are defined by culture but women who shape it instead. Women who believe that God is who He says He is and that He rewards those who earnestly seek Him (Hebrews 11:6 NIV).

> Let's not be women who are defined by culture but women who shape it instead.

Women who dare to stand up for what is good and right and holy. No matter what the cost.

Women who dare to move beyond ourselves and believe that God has called us to His kingdom for such a time as this.

Women who ground our identities not in the world's applause but in our heavenly Father's unconditional love for us.

"Christ came into the world for you," Ann Voskamp challenges us, "and you came into the world for Him."[5]

Don't you see the beauty of this? It's about God, not us! God is not looking for perfect women to work through; He's looking for His daughters who are all in. Totally committed to Him.

And we're not alone!

> God is not looking for perfect women to work through; He's looking for His daughters who are all in.

- "Greater is He who is in you than he who is in the world" (1 John 4:4 NASB).
- "Even as he [God] spoke, courage surged up within me" (Daniel 10:19).
- "Don't be afraid, don't waver. March out boldly . . . GOD is with you" (2 Chronicles 20:17).

The promises go on and on. This is our heritage and our spiritual foundation.

Heaven and earth are standing on tiptoes awaiting a Spirit-led, Spirit-intoxicated, Spirit-empowered woman. A woman who believes God is with her and in her and wants to work through her for His glory.

Will you join me in becoming a woman like that? Sure, this book is almost over, but the journey's only just begun. So be on the lookout—seek out like-minded, rebellious women around you. Ask God to bring mentors and older godly women into your life. Don't try to do it alone! Let's strike out together on a mission.

"We're being shown how to turn our backs on a godless, indulgent life, and how to take on a God-filled, God-honoring life. *This new life is starting right now*" (Titus 2:11; emphasis added).

Let's link arms—from bustling cities to small communities, college dorm rooms to coffee shops—and shout for all the world to hear, "As for me and my generation of women, we will serve the Lord!"

Don't mess with us.

With our God, we are rebellious. We are unstoppable. And we will change our world!

Notes

Chapter 1: A Cruel Joke

1. Steve Pokin, "Megan's Story," *St. Charles Journal*, November 13, 2007, http://www.meganmeierfoundation.org/ megans-story.html; Lauren Collins, "The Friend Game: Behind the Online Hoax That Led to a Girl's Suicide," *New Yorker*, January 21, 2008, 36–37, http://msl1.mit.edu/furdlog/ docs/newyorker_articles/2008-01-21_newyorker_ megan_meier.pdf.

2. "Parents: Cyber Bullying Led to Teen's Suicide," *ABC News*, November 19, 2007, http://abcnews.go.com/GMA/ story?id=3882520&page=1.

3. Kate Schwartz, "Criminal Liability for Internet Culprits: The Need for Updated State Laws Covering the Full Spectrum of Cyber Victimization," *Washington University Law Review*, 87 no. 2 (2009): 407–36.

4. Jennifer Steinhauer, "Woman Who Posed as Boy Testifies in Case That Ended in Suicide of 13-Year-Old," *New York Times*, November 20, 2008, http://www.nytimes.com/2008/11/21/ us/21myspace.html?_r=0.

5. Melissa Brock., "Operation Beautiful: The Story behind Our Song 'Courage,'" Superchick Online, February 22, 2010, http://www.superchickonline.com/2010/02/the-story- behind-our-song-courage/.

6. Ibid.

7. Ibid.

8. Ibid.

9. Ibid.

Chapter 2: Don't Drink the Kool-Aid

1. Sarah Petersen, "ABC's New Show 'Mistresses' Accused of Glamorizing Adultery," *Deseret News*, May 30, 2013, http://www.deseretnews.com/article/865580901/ABCs-new-show-Mistresses-accused-of-glamorizing-adultery.html?pg=all.

2. Candace Currie, Klaus Hurrelman, Wolfgang Settertobulte, Rebecca Smith, and Joanna Todd, eds., "Health and Health Behaviour among Young People," *WHO Policy Series: Health Policy for Children and Adolescents International Report*, 2010, http://www.euro.who.int/__data/assets/pdf_file/0006/119571/E67880.pdf.

3. Ibid.

4. "Hookup Survey Results," *Seventeen*, http://www.seventeen.com/health-sex-fitness/special/hookup-survey-results-hsp-0406.

5. Bill Albert, Sarah Brown, and Christine Flanigan, eds., "14 and Younger: The Sexual Behavior of Young Adolescents (Summary)," The National Campaign to Prevent Teen Pregnancy, 2003, http://thenationalcampaign.org/sites/default/files/resource-primary-download/ss3_youngadols.pdf.

6. Carolyn Coker Ross, "Why Do Women Hate Their Bodies?" 2012, *Psych Central* blog, http://psychcentral.com/blog/archives/2012/06/02/why-do-women-hate-their-bodies/.

7. "Poll: Have You Ever Wished You Could Surgically Change Something about Your Body?" *Seventeen*, October 1, 2007, http://www.seventeen.com/health-sex-fitness/special/plastic-surgery-poll-0807.

8. Sadie Whitelocks, "Mummy, Just What I Always Wanted! Girl, 7, Gets 7,000 Euro Liposuction Voucher for Christmas from 'Human Barbie' Mum," *Mail Online*, January 4, 2012, http://www.dailymail.co.uk/femail/article-2081674/Poppy-Burge-gets-liposuction-voucher-Human-Barbie-mum-Sarah-Christmas.html.

9. J. J. Heller, "What Love Really Means," *When I'm With You*, 2010, Stone Table Records, http://www.youtube.com/watch?v=PgGUKWiw7Wk.

10. *Oxford English Dictionary* (New York: Oxford University Press, 2013), s.v. "rebel."

11. Bryan Norman, as cited in John Leland, "Rebels with a Cross," *New York Times*, March 2, 2006, http://www.nytimes.com/2006/03/02/fashion/thursdaystyles/02rebels.html?_r=0

12. Donald Miller, as cited in Leland, "Rebels with a Cross."

13. This biblical story is retold from Luke 8:40–56. All direct quotations are taken from *The Message*.

Chapter 3: No Longer a Victim

1. "My Story," Moisom.com video, June 12, 2012, http://www.moisom.com/videos/testimony/.

2. Ibid.

3. Mo Isom, "Don't Cry, Daddy," *Faith in the Game*, July 3, 2011, http://faithinthegame.tumblr.com/post/7184085947/dont-cry-daddy-by-mo-isom.

4. Ibid.

5. "My Story," Moisom.com video.

6. Ibid.

7. Ibid.

8. "70 Million Americans Feel Held Back by Their Past," Barna Group, November 3, 2011, http://www.barna.org/culture-articles/532-70-million-americans-feel-held-back-by-their-past?q=identity.

9. "Child Sexual Abuse: What Parents Should Know," American Psychological Association, http://www.apa.org/pi/families/resources/child-sexual-abuse.aspx.

10. "Sexual Violence: Facts at a Glance," Centers for Disease Control and Prevention, 2012, http://www.cdc.gov/ViolencePrevention/pdf/sv-datasheet-a.pdf.

11. "Abortion in the United States," Guttmacher Institute, http://www.guttmacher.org/media/presskits/abortion-US/statsandfacts.html.

12. Mike Stobbe, "Domestic Violence: 1 in 4 American Women Attacked by Intimate Partner," *Huffington Post,* December 14, 2011, http://www.huffingtonpost.com/2011/12/15/domestic-violence-survey_n_1150158.html.

13. "Depression in Women," Mental Health America, http://www.mentalhealthamerica.net/conditions/depression-women#2.

14. "Eating Disorders Statistics," National Association of Anorexia Nervosa and Associated Disorders, http://www.anad.org/get-information/about-eating-disorders/eating-disorders-statistics/.

15. "Statistics on Sexually Transmitted Infections," American Sexual Health Association, http://www.ashasexualhealth.org/std-sti/std-statistics.html.

16. "Suicide in the U.S.: Statistics and Prevention," National Institute of Mental Health, http://www.nimh.nih.gov/health/publications/suicide-in-the-us-statistics-and-prevention/index.shtml.

17. This biblical story is retold from John 8:1–11. All direct quotations are taken from *The Message*.

18. Timothy Keller, *Counterfeit Gods: The Empty Promises of Money, Sex, and Power, and the Only Hope That Matters* (New York: Penguin, 2009), 88.

19. Brennan Manning, *The Ragamuffin Gospel: Good News for the Bedraggled, Beat-Up, and Burnt Out* (Sisters, OR: Multnomah, 2005), 115.

20. Ibid., 220.

21. Henri Nouwen, "The Wounded Healer," *Bread for the Journey* (HarperSanFrancisco, 1997).

22. Isom, "Don't Cry, Daddy."

23. Red, "Pieces," *End of Silence,* 2006, Essential Records, http://www.redmusiconline.com/end-of-silence.

Chapter 4: Dare to Believe

1. "Above and Beyond—Jen and Linda Barrick," *100 Huntley Street*, April 11, 2012, http://www.youtube.com/watch?v=MOt6OAUK8mM; Linda Barrick with John Perry, *Miracle for Jen: A Tragic Accident, a Mother's Desperate Prayer, and Heaven's Extraordinary Answer* (Carol Stream, IL: Tyndale, 2012), 82.

2. "The Jennifer Barrick Story," Hope Out Loud video, 9:01, http://www.youtube.com/watch?v=00pWA7mYW-A.

3. "The Miracle for Jen," Hope Out Loud video, 4:08, http://www.hopeoutloud.com/video.html.

4. For more information, visit www.ewomen.net.

5. "Three Spiritual Journeys of Millennials," Barna Group, May 9, 2013, https://www.barna.org/barna-update/teens-nextgen/612-three-spiritual-journeys-of-millennials#.UpTgTcSX86J.

6. Ibid.

7. Dietrich Bonhoeffer, *The Cost of Discipleship* (New York: Touchstone, 1995), 44.

8. This biblical story is retold from 1 Samuel 1–2. All direct quotations are taken from *The Message*.

9. "Three Spiritual Journeys of Millennials," Barna Group.

10. Bonhoeffer, *The Cost of Discipleship*, 44.

11. To read more about Jen's amazing testimony, check out *Miracle for Jen: A Tragic Accident, a Mother's Desperate Prayer, and Heaven's Extraordinary Answer* (Carol Stream, IL: Tyndale, 2012).

Chapter 5: I Am Woman

1. Mark Gray, "Miss Nebraska Becomes Miss America," *People*, January 16, 2011, http://www.people.com/people/article/0,,20458100,00.html.

2. Teresa Scanlan, "Miss America Is Here: Why Am I Competing?," Miss Nebraska 2010, http://teresastravelsandtidbits.blogspot.com/2011/01/miss-america-is-here-why-am-i-competing.html.

3. Ibid.

4. "New Miss America Says God Gives Her a Purpose," Faith News Network, January 18, 2011, http://www.faithnews.cc/?p=8520.

5. Margot Peppers, "'I Thought About Jumping Off a Mountain': Former Miss America Tells How Pressure and Criticism Over Her Looks After Winning the Title Made Her Contemplate Suicide," *Mail Online*, September 9, 2013, http://www.dailymail.co.uk/femail/article-2416046/Former-Miss-America-Teresa-Scanlan-reveals-pressure-criticism-winning.html.

6. Ibid.

7. Helen Reddy, "I Am Woman," *I Don't Know How to Love Him*, 1971, Capitol Records.

8. Hugh Rawson and Margaret Miner, eds., *The Oxford Dictionary of American Quotations* (New York: Oxford University Press US, 2005), 735.

9. Kim Kardashian, "A Message to My Fans," November 1, 2011, http://kimkardashian.celebuzz.com/2011/11/01/a-message-to-my-fans/.

10. Larry Crabb, "Whistle-blowing Women, Love-frozen Men: A Liberating Look at Gender," Presentation at 2011 AACC World Conference, Opryland Hotel, Nashville, Tennessee.

11. Ibid.

12. Eric and Leslie Ludy, *Wrestling Prayer: A Passionate Communion with God* (Eugene, OR: Harvest House, 2009), 6.

13. Ibid.

14. This biblical story is retold from Esther 1–7. All direct quotations are taken from the English Standard Version of the Bible.

15. Steven Garber, as cited in Kate Harris, *Wonder Women: Navigating the Challenges of Motherhood, Career, and Identity* (Grand Rapids, MI: Zondervan, 2013), 37.

16. Rebekah Lyons, "Why Are the Women Fading?" *Q Ideas,* http://old.qideas.org/blog/why-are-all-the-women-fading.aspx.

17. Jim Elliot, quoted in Elisabeth Elliot, *Through Gates of Splendor* (Carol Stream, IL: Tyndale, 1981), 20.

18. Lilian Calles Barger, *Eve's Revenge: Women and a Spirituality of the Body* (Grand Rapids, MI: Brazos Press, 2003), 118.

19. Grace Gold, "Miss America Teresa Scanlan Reveals Her Time-Saving Beauty Secrets," *Stylelist.com,* February 8, 2011, http://main.stylelist.com/2011/02/08/miss-america-teresa-scanlan-beauty-secrets/.

Chapter 6: Sex and Sexy

1. Christine Thomasos, "Lolo Jones Reconsiders Virginity Talk after Criticism from Teammates, Olympics Fans," *The Christian Post,* August 9, 2012, http://www.christianpost.com/news/lolo-jones-reconsiders-virginity-talk-after-criticism-from-teammates-olympics-fans-79757/.

2. Erin Malinowski, "The Most Popular Theory on Why Lolo Jones Didn't Medal at the Olympics," *Deadspin,* August 7, 2012, http://deadspin.com/5932782/the-most-popular-theory-on-why-lolo-jones-didnt-medal-at-the-olympics.

3. Thomasos, "Lolo Jones Reconsiders Virginity Talk."

4. "Lolo Jones until Marriage: Real Sports with Bryant Gumbel—Episode #182," *HBO Sports* video, 2:28, May 21, 2012, http://www.youtube.com/watch?feature=player_embedded&v=h_SRO9mpt4Y.

5. "Lolo Jones Overcomes Hurdles to Contend for Olympic Gold," *Access Hollywood,* August 19, 2008, http://www.accesshollywood.com/lolo-jones-overcomes-hurdles-to-contend-for-olympic-gold_article_10922.

6. "London 2012 Olympics: American Hurdler Lolo Jones Says Being a Virgin Is Harder than Training for Games," *The Telegraph*, May 23, 2012, http://www.telegraph.co.uk/sport/olympics/athletics/9284800/London-2012-Olympics-American-hurdler-Lolo-Jones-says-being-a-virgin-is-harder-than-training-for-Games.html.

7. "Lolo Jones until Marriage," *HBO Sports* video.

8. "AshleyMadison Offers $1 Million to Prove Tim Tebow Is NOT A Virgin," *Huffington Post,* April 25, 2012, http://www.huffingtonpost.com/2012/04/25/tim-tebow-virginity-ashleymadison-1-million_n_1452912.html.

9. Ibid.

10. Justin Garcia, Chris Reiber, Sean Massey, and Ann Merriwether, "Sexual Hook-Up Culture," *Monitor on Psychology* 44, no. 2 (February 2013), 60.

11. John Stossel, "Sex in Middle School?," *ABC News,* December 6, 2013, http://abcnews.go.com/2020/story?id=123789.

12. "American Opinion on Teen Pregnancy and Related Issues," National Campaign to Prevent Teen Pregnancy, May 2007, http://thenationalcampaign.org/resource/science-says-31.

13. Tamar Lewin, "Are These Parties for Real?," *New York Times*, June 30, 2005, http://www.nytimes.com/2005/06/30/fashion/thursdaystyles/30rainbow.html?pagewanted=all&_r=0.

14. "Hookup Survey Results," *Seventeen*, http://www.seventeen.com/health-sex-fitness/special/hookup-survey-results-hsp-0406.

15. Rachel Duke, "More Women Lured to Pornography Addiction," *Washington Times,* July 11, 2010, http://www.washingtontimes.com/news/2010/jul/11/more-women-lured-to-pornography-addiction/?page=all.

16. Dominique Mosbergen, "California Preschool, Rocked by Sex Scandal, Is Closing Its Doors," *Huffington Post,* February 3, 2013, http://www.huffingtonpost.com/2013/02/03/preschool-sex-scandal-california_n_2607512.html.

17. Juliet Macur and Nate Schweber, "Rape Case Unfolds on Web and Splits City," *New York Times,* December 16, 2012, http://www.nytimes.com/2012/12/17/sports/high-school-football-rape-case-unfolds-online-and-divides-steubenville-ohio.html?pagewanted=all.

18. Garcia, Reiber, Massey, and Merriwether, "Sexual Hook-Up Culture."

19. Ibid.

20. "Statistics on Sexually Transmitted Infections," American Sexual Health Association, http://www.ashasexualhealth.org/std-sti/std-statistics.html.

21. Candace Bushnell, *Sex and the City* (New York: Grand Central, 2006), 5–6.

22. Ibid., 5.

23. Ibid., 6.

24. "The Benefits of Marriage Brief," *The Heritage Foundation*; Christopher F. Scott and Susan Sprecher, "Sexuality in Marriage, Dating, and Other Relationships: A Decade Review," *Journal of Marriage and Family* 62, no. 4 (November 2000): 999–1017.

25. Linda Waite and Evelyn Lehrer, "The Benefits from Marriage and Religion in the United States: A Comparative Analysis," *Population*

and Development Review 29, no. 2 (June 2003): 255–76, http://www.ncbi.nlm.nih.gov/pmc/articles/PMC2614329/.

26. Gary Thomas, *Sacred Marriage: What If God Designed Marriage to Make Us Holy More Than to Make Us Happy?* (Grand Rapids, MI: Zondervan, 2002), 206.

27. This biblical story is retold from Song of Solomon 1–8. All direct quotations are taken from *The Message*.

28. Thomas, *Sacred Marriage*, 226.

29. Ibid., 206.

30. Doug Rosenau and Michael Todd Wilson, eds., *Soul Virgins: Redefining Single Sexuality* (Ada, MI: Baker, 2006), 36–37.

31. Erica Tan and Anna Maya, "Soul-Sexy Femininity," in Rosenau and Wilson, eds., *Soul Virgins,* 120.

32. Ibid., 121.

33. Find out more about *Verily* magazine and their company beliefs at www.verilymag.com.

34. "Verily Magazine's No-Photoshop Policy Proves It Can Be Done," *Huffington Post,* October 14, 2013, http://www.huffingtonpost.com/2013/10/10/verily-magazine-no-photoshop_n_4079217.html.

35. Tan and Maya, "Soul-Sexy Femininity," 119.

36. Ibid., 121.

Chapter 7: From Facebook to Face-to-Face

1. "Gabby Douglas Talks About Life After the Olympics!" *Perez TV,* 5:45, May 16, 2013, http://www.youtube.com/watch?v=u0SmxaHQmqY.

2. Ibid.

3. Ilyssa Pantiz, "Gabby Douglas's Mom Says She Is a Fighter," *MORE*, http://www.more.com/gabby-douglas-olympics-mom.

4. Samantha Bresnahan and James Masters, "Golden Gabby: How a Mother's Love Drove Olympic Champion Douglas," *CNN*, August 9, 2013, http://www.cnn.com/2013/08/07/sport/gabby-douglas-olympics-racism/.

5. Tony Rossi, "Grace, Gold & Glory: An Interview with Olympic Gold Medalist Gabrielle Douglas and Her Mom, Natalie Hawkins," *Patheos*, April 17, 2013, http://www.patheos.com/blogs/christophers/2013/04/grace-gold-glory-an-interview-with-olympic-gold-medalist-gabrielle-douglas-and-her-mom-natalie-hawkins/.

6. Ibid.

7. Daniel Bates, "Gabby Douglas Slams Her Gold Digger Father and Claims Former Gym Where Staff Told Her to 'Get a Nose Job' Almost Drove Her to Quit Gymnastics," *Mail Online*, August 30, 2012, http://www.dailymail.co.uk/news/article-2195978/Timothy-Douglas-Gabby-Douglas-slams-gold-digger-father-claims-gym-staff-told-nose-job-drove-quit.html.

8. Gabrielle Douglas and Michelle Burford, *Grace, Gold and Glory: My Leap of Faith* (Grand Rapids, MI: Zondervan, 2013), 6.

9. Rossi, "Grace, Gold & Glory."

10. Ann Oldenburg, "Gabby Douglas on Her Hair: 'Nothing is Going to Change,'" *USA Today*, August 6, 2012, http://content.usatoday.com/communities/entertainment/post/2012/08/gabby-douglas-on-her-hair-nothing-is-going-to-change/1#.UpjNicSX_kY.

11. Rossi, "Grace, Gold & Glory."

12. Douglas and Burford, *Grace, Gold and Glory*, 3.

13. Tracy Scott, "Gabrielle Douglas Talks Faith in New Book," *S2smagazine.com*, November 27, 2012, http://s2smagazine. com/21794/gabrielle-douglas-talks-faith-new-book/; Adelle Banks, "Olympian Gabby Douglas Talks Faith, Forgiveness and Matzo Ball Soup," *Religion News Service*, December 10, 2012, http://www.religionnews.com/2012/12/10/olympian-gabby-douglas-talks-faith-forgiveness-and-matzo-ball-soup/.

14. Elaine Quijano, "Olympic Champion Gabby Douglas a Hometown Hero to Aspiring Gymnasts," *CBS News*, August 3, 2012, http://www.cbsnews.com/news/olympic-champion-gabby-douglas-a-hometown-hero-to-aspiring-gymnasts/.

15. Emily Badger, "Yes, the Internet Is Taking Up Time You Used to Spend with Actual People," *The Atlantic*, October 23, 2013, http://www.theatlanticcities.com/arts-and-lifestyle/2013/10/yes-internet-taking-time-you-used-spend-actual-people/7326/.

16. Jay Baer, "Social Media, Pretend Friends, and the Lie of False Intimacy," *Convince & Convert*, http://www.convinceandconvert.com/social-networks/social-media-pretend-friends-and-the-lie-of-false-intimacy/.

17. Shauna Niequist, "Instagram's Envy Effect," *Relevant*, April 4, 2013, http://www.relevantmagazine.com/culture/tech/stop-instagramming-your-perfect-life.

18. This biblical story is retold from Ruth 1–4. All direct quotations are taken from *The Message*.

19. C. S. Lewis, *The Four Loves* (Orlando, FL: Hartcourt Brace & Company, 1960), 121.

20. Henry and Richard Blackaby, *Experiencing God Day by Day* (Nashville: B&H, 2006), 303.

21. Ann Voskamp, "How the Hidden Dangers of Comparison
     are Killing us . . . {and Our Daughters}: The Measuring Stick
     Principles," *Aholyexperience.com,* November 6, 2013,
     http://www.aholyexperience.com/2013/11/how-the-hidden-
     dangers-of-comparison-are-killing-us-and-our-daughters-the-
     measuring-stick-principle/.

Chapter 8: Something to Live For

1. Katie Davis, quoted in David Platt, "The Gospel and
     Materialism—Part 2," *Radical*, http://www.radical.net/media/
     series/view/842/Radical.net.
 2. "Katie Davis Speaks Part 1," Amazima Ministries video,
     14:01, November 30, 2010, http://www.youtube.com/
     watch?v=EqaphcYWBEQ.
 3. Ibid.
 4. "700 Club Interactive—October 13, 2011," *700 Club*, 4:01, October
     13, 2011, http://www.cbn.com/tv/1407014315001. Copyright 2011
     The Christian Broadcasting Network, Inc. Used with permission.
     All rights reserved.
 5. Katie Davis, quoted in David Platt, "The Gospel and
     Materialism—Part 2."
 6. Ibid.
 7. Personal communication with Katie Davis, March 5, 2014.
 8. "Kisses from Katie," Simon & Schuster video, 4:01, September 2,
     2011, http://www.youtube.com/watch?v=TY0YGrGZdR4#t=17.
 9. Katie Davis, quoted in David Platt, "The Gospel and
     Materialism—Part 2."
10. Ibid.
11. Ibid.

12. "Katie Davis Speaks Part 1," Amazima Ministries video.

13. Ibid.

14. Katie Davis, quoted in David Platt, "The Gospel and Materialism—Part 2."

15. Katie Davis with Beth Clark, *Kisses from Katie: A Story of Relentless Love and Redemption* (New York: Howard, 2012), xix.

16. "About Amazima Founder, Katie Davis," Amazima Ministries, http://www.amazima.org/katiesstory.html.

17. "Katie Davis Speaks Part 2," Amazima Minstries video, 2:09, November 30, 2010, http://www.youtube.com/watch?v=ui4xZP2TQjk.

18. Davis with Clark, *Kisses from Katie,* xix.

19. Michelle Healy, "Millennials Might Not Be So Special After All, Study Finds," *USA Today,* March 3, 2012, http://usatoday30.usatoday.com/news/health/wellness/story/2012-03-15/Millennials-might-not-be-so-special-after-all-study-finds/53552744/1.

20. Joel Stein, "Millennials: The Me Me Me Generation," *Time,* May 20, 2013, http://content.time.com/time/magazine/article/0,9171,2143001,00.html.

21. Elisabeth Eaves, "Azar Nafisi on the American Dream," *Forbes,* March 22, 2007, http://www.forbes.com/2007/03/21/azar-nafisi-dream-oped-cx_ee_dream0307_0322nafisi.html.

22. Davis with Clark, *Kisses from Katie,* xx–xi.

23. This biblical story is retold from Luke 1 and John 19. All direct quotes are taken from *The Message.*

24. Henry Blackaby and Claude V. King, *Experiencing God: Knowing and Doing the Will of God* (Nashville: LifeWay, 1990), chapter 6.

25. "700 Club Interactive—October 13, 2011," *700 Club.*

Chapter 9: Rebel and Be Set Free

1. Mrs. Howard Taylor, *Borden of Yale* (Philadelphia: China Inland Mission, 1926), 148.
2. Ibid., ix.
3. Howard Culbertson, "No Reserves. No Retreats. No Regrets.," *Southern Nazarene University*, 2002, https://home.snu.edu/~hculbert/regret.htm.
4. Christian Smith, "Finding the Devoted Generation," *MORF*, http://morfmagazine.com/article/finding-devoted-generation.
5. Ann Voskamp, *The Greatest Gift: Unwrapping the Full Love Story of Christmas* (Carol Stream, IL: Tyndale, 2013), 258.

About the Author

Megan Clinton (now Megan Clinton Allison) graduated from Liberty University with a degree in Pre-Med/Biology and is currently attending Physician Assistant (PA) School at Jefferson College of Health Sciences. As part of the Extraordinary Women travel team with her mom, Julie Clinton, Megan has a passion to see young women find their identity in Christ, be set free, and live God's dream for their lives. In addition, she is excited to be equipped as a PA to provide medical care to those in need through international mission work.

Megan is the author of *Totally God's* (with her dad, Dr. Tim Clinton), *Totally God's 4 Life Devotional,* and *Smart Girls, Smart Choices: Avoiding the 10 Biggest Mistakes Young Women Make* (with Laura Captari). Megan was recently married to the love of her life and high school sweetheart, Ben. They have a teacup Yorkie named Bella.

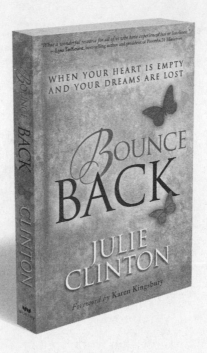

WORTHY
PUBLISHING

IF YOU ENJOYED THIS BOOK, WILL YOU CONSIDER
SHARING THE MESSAGE WITH OTHERS?

- Mention the book in a Facebook post, Twitter update, Pinterest pin, blog post, or upload a picture through Instagram.

- Recommend this book to those in your small group, book club, workplace, and classes.

- Head over to facebook.com/worthypublishing, "Like" the page, and post a comment as to what you enjoyed the most.

- Tweet "I recommend reading #BeRebellious by @megannclinton // @worthypub"

- Pick up a copy for someone you know who would be challenged and encouraged by this message.

- Write a book review online.

You can subscribe to Worthy Publishing's
newsletter at worthypublishing.com.

WORTHY PUBLISHING
FACEBOOK PAGE

WORTHY PUBLISHING
WEBSITE